The Second Register Book Of The Parish Church Of Saint Mary, Horncastle: For Marriages, Christenings, And Burials

John Clare Hudson

The Second

Register Book

OF THE

Parish Church of Saint Mary,

Horncastle,

FOR

Marriages, Christenings & Burials,

From March 25th, 1640, to December 6th,
1685.

Edited by the

REV. J. CLARE HUDSON, M.A.

Horncastle:
MDCCCXCVI.

E. Wo

HORNCASTLE :

W. K. MORTON,

1896.

PREFACE.

The Second Register Book of Horncastle, wholly comprised in this Volume, now and then gives evidence of the stormy period of the great Civil War and the brief interlude of the Commonwealth. The entry of burial of Sir Ingram Hopton, Kt., October 13, 1643 (p.9.), who was slain at the Battle of Winceby, is the first record we have of the Civil War; and on the same page we have entries of the burial of the various soldiers. It was soon after this event that the Rev. Thomas Gibson, Vicar, was "outed of Horncastle by Cromwell's Commissioners" (see p. 102 of the printed volume of the First Register Book). As the account of his sufferings, as related by Mr. John Walker in his book entitled, "An Attempt towards recovering an Account of the Numbers and Sufferings of the Clergy of the Church of England, Heads of Colleges, Fellows, Scholars, &c., who were Sequestered, Harrassed, &c., in the late Times of the Great Rebellion. London, 1714 fol.," p. 252, is so interesting, we give it *in extenso.*

"LINCOLNSHIRE. GIBSON, THOMAS, A. M. *Horn-Castle,* V. This very worthy Person was Born at *Keswick,* in *Cumberland,* and Educated at *Queen's-College* in *Oxford;* where he continued till he took the Degrees in Arts; and then returning into his own Country, was preferred to the *Free School* of *Carlisle,* and from thence to that of *Newcastle;* both which he managed with great Reputation several Years; and was from the Latter of them Promoted by the Bishop of *Carlisle* to the *Vicaridge* of *Horn-Castle,* in the Year 1654.

"That which most expos'd him to the Fury of the Party, was a Sermon Preach'd at the Election for the *Convocation* in 1640; which they could never forgive him; and therefore made him the first Instance of their Rage in those Parts. For about the Beginning of 1643, they Seized, and carried him away Prisoner to *Hull,* where he lay three or four Months. After which returning to his *Vicaridge,* some of his *Factious Parishioners* Articled against him for *Ormanism* (meaning *Arminianism,* and doubtless understood it very well, tho' they would not call it by the right Name) for which however, he was committed to the County-Jayl at *Lincoln,* till he was at last Exchanged for a *Presbyterian Minister* at *Newark.* After this, in the Year 1644, Colonel *K——*, the Governor of *Boston* for the Parliament, gave Orders for a Party of Horse to go and fetch him Prisoner, and *Plunder his House;* but John *Lillbourn,* (who had been his *Scholar,* and was then Lieutenant-Colonel to Colonel *King*), affirming upon his own Knowledge, that he was a *Good and Godly Man,* got the Order, with much ado, suspended for the present: But *Lillbourn* afterwards, upon some *Disagreement* with his *Colonel,* going to *London,* the Order was again Revived, and Mr. *Gibson* made a Prisoner, his *House Plundered,* and his Saddle-Horse, his Draught-Horses, and his Oxen *taken from him.* He continu'd a *Prisoner at Boston some considerable time,* and was but just *dismissed* from thence, before he was *again Seised,* and carried Prisoner (a 2d time) to *Lincoln-Jayl;* from whence he had been *dismiss'd but Six Months* before. After this he was again taken up by a *Party* of *Horse,* and carried Prisoner to *Tattors-Hall-Castle,* where he had *very Ill Usage* for 17 Weeks; and when he was at last *dismissed* from *this Confinement* also, he could not return to Reside at his Parish, as formerly; because he was *now*

Sequestred, and found an * *Intruder possess'd* of it. This being done, as I apprehend, *during his Confinement*, 'tis plain that he could *not have a Hearing*, much less his *Accusers Face to Face*, and *plead for* himself. The *Sentence* was passed by the *E.* of *M. August the 7th*, 1664. And the Substance of what he was *Charged* with, was his paying Obedience to the Rules and Orders of the *Church ;* defending *Episcopacy ;* and saying that he wondered any one, that believed St. *Paul's Epistles* should *Oppose it ; Preaching* up to the *Possibility* of Falling from Grace; refusing *Lecturers,* and the *Covenant ;* Scandalizing *Godly Ministers,* saying that *Prinn, Burton,* and *Bastwick Suffer'd Justly ;* as also that if Sir *John Hotham* did not fear the *King's Cannon,* he might well enough fear the Sentence of *Damnation* pronounced *Romans* the *13th ;* and calling the *Scots Rebels.* After this he betook himself to a *Mean House* about a Mile distant from *Horne-Castle ;* where *he,* and *his Wife,* and *Six Children lived very poorly ; and indeed must have Begged,* or *Starved,* for about *two Years,* but that he supported himself by teaching a few *Scholars.* At length he was made *Master* of the *Free-School* at *Newark,* from whence after two Years more, he removed to the *School* at *Sleeford* in this *County,* being presented to it by the *Lady Carr :* There he lived until the *Restoration,* and then *Re-assumed* his *Vicaridge,* in which he continued till his Death *Anno 1674,* in the *84th* Year of his *Age. He was a grave and venerable Person, of a Sober and Regular Conversation, and so Studious of Peace,* that when any Differences arose in his Parish he never rested till he had *Composed* them. He had likewise so well *Principled* his *Parish,* that of *250* Families in it, he left but *one* of them *Dissenters,* at his Death."

It will be noticed that Mr. Walker infers that the "intruded" Vicar, during these troublous times, was Mr. Obadiah How, whose name appears in an entry on folio 32*b* (p. 38 of this vol.) as marrying Jo: Smith and Abigail Hussey, on March 15, 1657. There is, I fear, no other evidence direct or indirect of this Minister.

The "Apology" of Mr. John Harding, Parish Clerk on fol. 21*a* (p. 24) is extremely interesting. He must have been a worthy member of that ancient craft, as he seems to have taken every care of these valuable Parish Records, writing up each entry in a clear legible hand. His burial is recorded on p. 56. May his worthy successor—Mr. John Coats Osborne, the present Parish Clerk, who entered on his office May 20th, 1847, and whose knowledge of the events which have happened in the Town and District is unsurpassed—live yet many years, and may he not omit to leave in a documentary Record some account of the history of the Town and District since the time he has known it, for the benefit of his fellow townsmen, by whom he is so universally respected.

The Contracts of Marriage which appear on pp. 26, 28, 29, 32, 34, 36, 38, and 41, are very interesting, as they carry out to the letter the Act of Parliament passed on August 24th, 1653 (see Burn's *Hist. of Parish Registers,* 1862, pp. 26-29, where the Act is fully quoted from Scobell's *Acts of Parliament,* 1658).

The third Register Book which is now in progress of publication in the Horncastle *Parish Magazine,* will in due course appear as the third volume of this printed series.

Thornton Vicarage,   J. CLARE HUDSON.
   Horncastle,
     June, 1896.

---

* *Who that was I know not ; but in 1668 one Obad. How got this Living.*

THE SECOND REGISTER BOOK.

DESCRIPTION.—The Second Book comprises entries from March 25th, 1640, to December 6th, 1683, and is wholly written on parchment. It measures 15in. by 5½in., and contains 67 folios or 134 pages; it is quite intact, no folios missing. The general condition is excellent, and the entries are all legible.

[Fol. 1a.]

Anno Decemo Sexto
Caroli Regis
1640.

A true Register of all the Christenings, Marriages, and Burials within the Parrish of Horncastle, vis :—

CHRISTENINGS.	[1640.]
Brisko, Bridget, *d.* John and Annie Brisko *c*	5 April
Snoden, Thomas, *s.* Rutland Snoden, Esqre. and Frances his wife *c*	7 ,,
Skelton, James *s.* James and Dorothie Skelton, *c*	12 ,,
Bitchfield, Ann *d.* John and Margaret Bitchfield, *c*	15 ,,
Castledine, Mary, *d.* Roger and Mary Castledine *c*	17 ,,
Smith, Elizabeth, *d.* John Smith, taylor *c*	19 ,,
Clark, Ann, *d.* William and Ann Clark *c*	26 ,,
Holbich, Edmond, *s.* Edmond and Ann Holbich *c*	2 May
Browne, Thomas, *s.* Thomas and Elizabeth Browne *c*	3 ,,
Tayler, Francis, *s.* Francis and Grace Tayler *c*	10 ,,
Snoden, Abigail, *d.* M^r. Scroope Snoden and Elizabeth his wife *c*	10 ,,
Tuke, Mary, *d.* Mary Tuke, a stranger *c*	15 ,,
Wright, George, *s.* George and Mary Wright *c*	17 ,,
Lames, Thomas, *s.* Robert and Ann Lames *c*	17 ,,
Watson, Dorothy, *d.* William and Elizabeth Watson *c*	17 ,,
Lawe, John, *s.* George and Esther Lawe *c*	14 June
Hamerton, William, *s.* William and Dorothie Hamerton, *c*	18 ,,
Dennys, John, *s.* Charles and Elizabeth Dennys *c*	21 ,,
Chapman, Thomas, son of Thomas Chapman, deceased and Mary his wife *c*	28 ,,
Markby, Elizabeth, *d.* George and Ann Markby *c*	28 ,,
Nelsey, Elizabeth, *d.* John and Elizabeth Nelsey *c*	4 July
Westeby, Katherine, *d.* Edward and Katherine Westeby *c*	26 ,,
Bunting, Jane, *d.* John and Elizabeth Bunting *c*	26 ,,
Fitch, John, *s.* John and Ellen Fitch *c*	13 Aug.
Thornton, Robert, *s.* M^r. John Thornton and Faith his wife *c*	30 ,,

[Fol. 1b.]

Barnard, Thomas, *s.* Robert and Martha Barnard *c*	30 ,,
Leach, William, *s* Richard and Sarah Leach *c*	31 ,,
Pinder, Elizabeth, *d.* Peter and Elizabeth Pinder *c*	13 Sept.
Mackris, Elizabeth, *d.* Christopher and Elizabeth Mackris *c.*	13 ,,
Palmer, Robert, *s.* John and Ann Palmer *c*	27 ,,
Francis, John, *s.* John Francis the younger and Frances his wife *c*	5 Oct.
Surflet, Richard, *s.* Robert and Ann Surflet *c*	18 ,,

Spinkes, Mary, *d.* John and Alice Spinkes *c*	1 Nov.
Goulsborrow, John, *s.* William and Martha Goulsborrow *c*	4 ,,
Richardson, Ann, *d.* John and Mary Richardson *c*	8 ,,
Burch, Elizabeth, *d.* Thomas and Elizabeth Burch *c*	8 ,,
Graves, Samuell, *s.* Lawrence and Ann Graves *c*	28 .?
Broughton, Mary, *d.* Edward and Ann Broughton *c*	6 Dec.
Kerk, Ann, *d.* William and Ann Kerk *c*	8 ,,
West, John, *s.* Lyonell and Alice West *c*	13 ,,
Nicholls, Bridget, *d.* Thomas and Elizabeth Nicholls *c*	20 ,,
Chapman, Mary, *d.* John and Mary Chapman *c*	27 ,,
Mackris, Ellen, *d.* Edward and Barbara Mackris *c*	2 Feb.
Clarke, Susanna, *d.* Thomas and Susanna Clarke *c*	2 ,,
Blansherd, Katherine, *d.* John and Katherine Blanshard *c*	7 ,,
Lill, Mary, *d.* Thomas and Margaret Lill *c*	7 ,,
Wright, John, *s.* John and Mary Wright *c*	15 ,,
Vinter, Richard, *s.* Richard and Mary Vinter *c*	16 ,,
Beverley, Georhe, *s.* John and Ciciley Beverley *c*	18 ,,
Richardson, James, *s.* Thomas and Elizabeth Richardson *c*	21 ,,
Wooding, Anne, *d.* Phillip and Ellen Wooding *c*	21 ,,
Parkins, Magdalen, *d.* Robert and Elizabeth Parkins *c*	28 ,,
Pasmore, Elizabeth, *d.* William and Mary Pasmore *c*	7 Mar.
Bradley, Richard, *s.* Richard and Elizabeth Bradley *c*	12 ,,

[Fol. 2a.]

Johnson, Mary, *d.* John and Frances Johnson *c*	14 ,,
Enderby, John, *s.* Thomas and Margaret Enderby *c*	14 ,,

MARRIAGES, 1640.

White, Charles	} *m*	
Tarbles, Bridget		2 April
Cayler, Lawrence	} *m*	
Burle, Mary		30 ,,
Saldam, Edward	} *m*	
Smith, Elizabeth		4 June
Stanforth, John	} *m*	
Mathers, Mary		13 Aug.
Gundy, Thomas	}	
Harrison, Mary		28 Sept.
Quenningborrow, John	} *m* wth. a Lycense	
[blank], Elizabeth		
Stake, Thomas	} *m*	
Scarborough, Ellen		14 Jan.
Barkby, Richard	} *m*	
Beverley, Ann		3 Feb.
Burton, Luke	} *m*	
Hamerton, Mary		4 ,,

BURIALS, 1640.

Simpkin, John *b*	25 Mar.
Fisher, Dorothie, widow *b*	28 ,,
Lill, Mary, infant *b*	30 ,,
Smith, Elizabeth, spinster, *b*	31 ,,
Bradley, Thomas, infant *b*	2 April
Mayes, Robert, baker *b*	6 ,,
Leachman, Thomas, blacksmith *b*	15 ,,
Skelton, Faith, infant *b*	20 ,,
Westerby, Edward, infant *b*	23 ,,
Childe, Anthony *b*	26 ,,
Minting, Isabel *b*	26 ,,
Clarke, Mary *b*	11 May
Stanforth, Ann *b*	12 ,,

Snoden, Thomas, infant *b*	16	May
Davenporte, Jane *b*	21	,,
Belton, Thomas *b*	22	,,
Gregory, Henry *b*	11	June
Stanforth, Ann, infant *b*	17	,,
Tuke, Mary, infant *b*	17	,,
Hamerton, William, infant *b*	27	,,
Dennys, John, infant *b*	28	,,
Nelsey, John *b*	4	July
Lill, Alice *b*	16	Aug.
Portes, Grace *b*	29	,,
Johnson, Dorothie *b*	14	Sept.
Tayler, Robert, the elder *b*	20	,,
Guising, Sarah *b*	24	,,
Kerke, Thomas *b*	26	,,
Slater, Ellen *b*	28	,,
Lill, Solomon, infant *b*	2	Oct.
Barrow, Frances, infant *b*	21	,,
Tayler, Dorothie, widow *b*	30	,,

[Fol. 2*b*.]

Surflet, Richard, infant *b*	20	Nov
Leachman, Rosamond, infant *b*	29	,,
Surflet, Margaret *b*	14	Dec.
Richardson, Ann *b*	26	,,
Chapman, Mary *b*	28	,,
Snelland, Margaret *b*	22	,,
Brisco, Bridget *b*	18	Feb.
Lawson, John *b*	19	,,
Palmer, Mary, infant *b*	28	,,
Vinter, Richard, infant *b*	5	Mar.
Packris, Ellen, infant *b*	10	,,
Pasmore, Elizabeth *b*	11	,,

CHRISTENINGS, 1641.

Atkinson, John, *s.* Thomas and Rosamond Atkinson *c*	[1641.]	
	25	Mar.
Holderness, Sara, *d.* John and Joane Holderness *c*	28	,,
Tothdy, Magdalen, *d.* Thomas and Dorothie Tothby *c*	28	,,
Bromley, Grace, *d.* John and Isabel Bromley *c*	11	April
Salmon, {Robert, Thomas,} *ss.* George and Esther Salmon *c*	12	,,
Tayler, Elizabeth, *d.* Richard and ——— *c*	2	May
Mayer, Sarah, *d.* Thomas and Sarah Mayer *c*	8	,,
Newman, Susanna, *d.* William and Mary Newman *c*	9	,,
Vintner, Elizabeth, *d.* Adam and Jane Vintner *c*	9	,,
Gillam, William, *s.* Thomas and Jane Gillam *c*	9	,,
Gibson, Mary, *d.* Robert and Mary Gibson *c*	16	,,
Gibson, Margery, *d.* William and Susanna Gibson *c*	23	,,
Hutchinson, Charles, *s.* John and Mary Hutchinson *c*	4	June
Attenell, Elizabeth, *d.* Edward and Alice Attenell *c*	5	,,
Wells, Robert, *s.* Thomas and Mary Wells (glover) *c*	6	,,
Ledall, Mary, *d.* John and Martha Ledall *c*	13	,,
Lathropp, Susanna, *d.* John and Sarah Lathropp *c*	15	,,
Bridgett, Powderill, *d.* Richard and Mary Bridgett *c*	24	,,
Martingdale, Robert, *s.* Christopher and Mary Martingdale *c*	8	July
Skelton, Anne, *d.* John and Dorothy Skelton *c*	11	,,
Darby, John, *s.* Robert and Bridget Darby *c*	15	,,

[Fol. 3*a*.]

Garthside, Elizabeth, *d.* Francis and Ann Garthside	18	,,
Sampson, John, *s.* John and Ann Sampson	31	,,

Boulton, Lucy, d. John and Mary Boulton c   1 Aug.
Shotten, Lawrence, s. Charles and Alice Shotten c   15 ,,
Marley, Susanna, d. Henry and Ann Marley c   17 ,,
Hamerton, Robert, s. Robert and Margery Hamerton c   19 ,,
White, Robert, s. Charles and Bridget White c   22 ,,
Parkins, Elisabeth, d. Anthony and Katherine Parkins c   22 ,,
Moyser, Ann, d. Edwin and Julian Moyser c   25 ,,
Davenport, Susanna, d William and Susanna Davenport c   27 ,,
Lawson, Thomas, s. John and Ellen Lawson c   11 Sept.
Tayler, Ann, d. Lorence and Margaret Tayler c   21 ,,
Fitch, Robert, s. John and Ellen Fitch c   7 Oct.
Bonner, William, s. William and Isabel Bonner c   7 ,,
Benton, Thomas, s. Thomas and Joan Benton c   10 ,,
Baldan, Ann, d. Edward and Elisabeth Baldan c   20 ,,
Lopsit, John, s. Thomas and Mary Lopsit c   7 Nov
Tayler, Mary, d. Francis and Grace Tayler c   7 ,,
Pinder, Susanna, d. Peter and Elizabeth Pinder c   14 ,,
Burton, Sarah, d. Luke and Mary Burton c   18 ,,
Markby, Ann, d. Richard and Ann Markby c   21 ,,
Snowden, William, s. Rutland and Frances Snowden c   25 ,,
Wright, John, s. George and Margaret Wright c   28 ,,
Coupland, John, s. George and Katherine Coupland c   19 Dec.
Tharrold, James, s. Thomas and Margaret Tharrold c   25 ,,
Willyman, Gilbert, s. Gilbert and Margaret Willyman c   26 ,,
Gersam, Hester, d. Hugh and Elizabeth Gersam c   6 Jan.
Richardson, John, s. John and Margery Richardson c   16 ,,
Pogson, John, s. Robert and Katherine Pogson c   23 ,,
Pasmore, Elizabeth, d. William and Mary Pasmore c   3 Feb.
Shepherd, Elizabeth, d. Walter and Katherine Shepherd c   6 ,,
Minting, Elizabeth, d. Edward and ——— Minting c   12 ,,

[Fol. 3b.]

Walsher, Alice, d. John and Elizabeth Walsher c   27 ,,
Goake, Isabel, d. John and Anthony Goake c   4 Mar.
Abbot, Mary, d. Richard and Elizabeth Abbot c   4 ,,
Portes, William, s. George and Dorothie Portes c   13 ,,
Surflet, John, s. Robert and Ann Surflet c   15 ,,
Lawe, George, s. George and Esther Lawe c   17 ,,
Tayler, Mary, d. Robert and Margaret Tayler c   17 ,,
Maultby, Mary, d. William and Elizabeth Maultby c   25 ,,

MARRIAGES, 1641.

Goake, John }
Stamp, Aulterie } m   4 May
Snoddall, Christopher }
Rushby, Isabell } m   4 ,,
Portes, George }
Johnson, Dorothy } m   4 ,,
Welcher, John }
Spoure, Elizabeth } m   6 ,,
Shepherd, Walter }
Ward, Katherine } m   11 ,,
Alice, Thomas }
Greensmith, Dorothy } m   13 ,,
Parrish, John }
Arnold, Margaret } m   21 ,,
Soble, Thomas }
Mayes, Elizabeth } m   22 June
Portor, Robert }
White, Katherine } m   1 July

Redthorne, Thomas } *m*		8 Aug.
Conham, Elizabeth }		
Davenport, William } *m*		28 ,,
Mathews, Susanna }		
Simpson, Thomas } *m*		31 ,,
Lindley, Mary }		
Cotten, Robert } *m*		4 Oct.
Coupland, Alice }		
Daunse, Stephen } *m*		5 ,,
Hamerton, Mary }		
Lee, Henry } *m*		1 Nov.
Spurr, Diana }		
Burr, Edward } *m*		1 ,,
Cooke, Ann }		
West, John } *m*		25 ,,
Clarke, Mary }		

BURIALS, 1641.

Holderness, Sarah, infant *b*	29 Mar.
Rands, Margaret, spinster *b*	2 April
Salmon, Thomas, infant *b*	14 ,,
Bonner, George, paintter *b*	18 ,,
Salmon, Robert, infant *b*	19 ,,
Peares, Thomas, adolescens *b*	22 ,,
Smith, Luce, widow *b*	15 May
Winter, Elizabeth, infant *b*	16 ,,
Bartrom, Mary, widow *b*	19 ,,
Chapman, Mary, widow *b*	21 ,,
Page, Thomas *b*	25 ,,
Bandin, Nicholas *b*	26 ,,
Sanders, Richard *b*	6 June
Attenell, Elizabeth *b*	6 ,,
Graves, Martha *b*	21 ,,
Knole, Elizabeth *b*	18 July
Wright, Thomas, *als.* Balderston *b*	22 ,,

[Fol. 4a.]

Sampson, John, infant *b*	6 Aug.
Hamerton, Robert, infant *b*	20 ,,
Lawson, Thomas, infant *b*	18 Sept.
Parkins, Elizabeth, infant *b*	20 ,,
Nelsey, Bridget *b*	80 ,,
Fitch, Robert, infant *b*	8 Oct.
Wright, Ann, spinster *b*	18 ,,
Baledam, Ann, infant *b*	27 ,,
West, Elizabeth, widow *b*	2 Jan.
Lawnder, Elizabeth, spinster *b*	4 ,,
Lettis, Elizabeth *b*	18 ,,
Wright, Ann, infant *b*	22 ,,
Wright, John, infant *b*	24 ,,
Bradley, Richard, Laborer *b*	10 Feb.
Colling, Robert, adolescens *b*	22 ,,
Dimsdale, Christopher *b*	7 Mar.

CHRISTENINGS, 1642.

Tisdalle, Thomas, *s.* Robt. and Margaret Tisdaile *c*	29 ,,
Broughton. John, *s.* William and Isabell Broughton *c*	3 April
Maultby, Elizabeth, *d.* Thomas and Jane Moultby *c*	8 ,,
Soble, Thomas, *s.* Thomas and Elizabeth Sobie *c*	7 ,,
Leach, Richard, *s.* Richard and Sarah Leach *c*	15 ,,
Redthorne, Elizabeth, *d.* Thomas and Mary Redthorne *c*	9 May

Dimsdale, Thomas c	29 May
Simpson, Elizabeth, d. Thomas and Mary Simpson c	5 June
Harriss, Richard, s. Richard Harriss, of Drainfield in the County of Darby c	14 ,,
Beverley, Edward, s. John Beverley c	16 ,,
Donge, Edward, putative of Robt. Donge, of Tetforth c	18 ,,
Gunby, Robert, s. Thomas Gunby c	26 ,,
Lee, Robert and Richard, ss Henry Lee c	27 ,,
Vinter, Edward, s. Edward Vinter c	28 ,,
Groome, Thomas, s. George Groome c	16 July
Pringlesworth, Edward, s. Edward Pringlesworth c	19 ,,
Smith, Dorothie, d. John Smith, taylor c	7 Aug.
Burch, William, s. Thomas Burch c	12 ,,
Vrie, Elizabeth, d. Thomas Vrie c	16 ,,

[Fol. 4b.]

Wilkinson, John, s. Harbert Wilkinson c	28 ,,
Mason, Katherine, d. Nicholas Mason c	28 ,,
Daunse, George, s. Stephen Daunse c	4 Sept.
Parish, John, s. John Parish c	11 ,,
Leedale, John, s. John Leedale c	11 ,,
Nicholls, Susan, d. Thomas Nicholls c	25 ,,
Chapman, Anne, d. John Chapman c	27 ,,
Waide, Alice, d. Edward Waide c	2 Oct.
Butcher, Mary, d. Robt. Butcher c	6 ,,
Hamerton, John, s. Robt. Hamerton c	20 ,,
Mackris, Francis, s. Edward Mackris c	18 Nov.
Francis, John, s. Harmon Francis c	20 ,,
Baledam, Anne, d. Edward Baledam c	27 ,,
Fitch, William, s. John Fitch c	18 Dec.
Clark, John, s. William Clark c	20 ,,
Moyser, John, s. Edward Moyser c	4 Jan.
Johnson, Margery, d. John Johnson c	6 ,,
Chantry, Ann, bastard childe to Ann Chantry c	7 ,,
Burton, Nathaniell, s. Luke Burton c	19 ,,
Pinder, Elizabeth, d. Peter Pinder c	22 ,,
Blansherd, Bryan, s. John Blansherd, als. Briggs c	5 Feb.
Castledine, Elizabeth, d. Roger Castledine c	5 ,,
Gibson, Danyell, s. Mr. Thomas Gibson, Vicar of Horncastle c	9 ,,
Tayler, Mary, d. Richard Tayler c	23 ,,
Vinter, Isabell, d. Ann Vinter c	23 ,,
Westerby, Faith, d. Edward Westerby c	23 ,,
Enderby, Sarah, d. Thomas Enderby c	3 Mar.
Bromley, John, s. John Bromley c	5 ,,
Smith, Edward, s. John Smith c	5 ,,
Wooding, Thomas, s. Philip Wooding c	7 ,,
Lettis, Richard, s. Richard Lettis c	12 ,,
Crafte, Elizabeth, d. Henry Crafte c	21 ,,

[Fol. 5a.]

MARRIAGES, 1642.

Ruffells, John Bradley, Margaret } m	14 June
Sneddall, Christopher Wattam, Katherine } m	9 Aug.
Burton, Mathew Attenell, Mary } m	22 Sept.
Nelsey, John Lincoln, Pretazie } m	19 Jan.
Pinches, Thomas Shotten, Elizabeth } m	26 ,,

BURIALLS. 1642.

- Boyes, Robte. b	25 June
- Lindley, Elisabeth b	27 ,,
- Wright, John, infant b	7 April
- Atteneil, Thomas b	21 ,,
- Pasmore, Elizabeth, infant b	24 ,,
- Hutchinson, William, infant b	28 ,,
. Spinkes, Alice b	25 May
- Smith, William, adolescence b	27 ,,
- Sneddall, Isabell b	31 ,,
- Bradley, Elizabeth, infant b	12 June
- Redthorn, Elizabeth, infant b	15 ,,
- Enderby, Ann b	18 ,,
- Slater, Thomas b	21 ,,
- Lee, Robert, infant b	28 ,,
- Richard, —— infant b	30 ,,
- Beverley, Edward, infant b	12 July
. Vinter, Edward, infant b	27 ,,
- Burch, William infant b	14 Aug.
- Graves, Frances, infant b	8 Sept.
- Darby, Mary, infant b	9 ,,
- Kerk, Elizabeth b	22 ,,
- Wright, Susanna b	10 Oct.
- Browne, Robert b	12 ,,
- Leach, Richard, infant b	18 ,,
- Smith, Ann, *wife* John Smith, Iron. b	8 Nov.
- Mackris, Frances, infant b	30 ,,
- Smith, John, Ironmonger b	5 Dec.
- Wright, John, Labourer b	12 ,,
- Fitch, William, infant b	16 ,,
. Skelton, Mary b	23 ,,
- Peak, William b	29 ,,
- Maultby, Elizabeth b	22 Jan.
- Holbich, Edmond, infant b	17 Feb.
- Wells, Thomas, Senior, Tanner b	24 ,,
- Browne, Katherine, *widow* b	9 Mar.
- Baxter, Thomas, Cordwainer b	13 ,,
- Enderbie, Sarah, infant b	14 ,,

[Fol. 5b.]

CHRISTENINGS, 1643.

- Snoden, Thomas, s. Mr. Rutland Snoden c	6 April
- Powtherill, Thomas, s. Richard Powtherill c	9 ,,
- Bitchfield, William, s. John Bitchfield c	18 ,,
- Mackris, Mary, d. Christopher Mackris c	25 ,,
- Tayler, Lawrence, s. Lawrence Tayler c	30 ,,
- Skelton, John, s. James Skelton c	7 May
- Tayler, Ann, d. Thomas Tayler c	7 ,,
- Burch, Faith, d. John Burch c	14 ,,
- Gibson, Thomas, s. William Gibson c	21 ,,
- Graves. Martha, d. Lawrence Graves c	22 ,,
. Wright, John, s. George Wright c	28 ,,
- Clark, Thomas, s. Thomas Clarke c	6 June
- Gibson, John, s. Robert Gibson c	11 ,,
- Pasmore, Katherine, d. William Pasmore c	11 ,,
- Hancock, Elizabeth, d. Stephen Hancock c	11 ,,
- Bunting, Joshua, s. John Bunting c	12 ,,
- Mackris, William, s. Richard Mackris c	13 ,,
- Chappell, Gabriel, bastard child of Alice Chappelle c	24 ,,

Lawrence, Hollingshead, s Robert Lawrence c	8 July
Kerk, Judeth, d William Kerk c	9 ,,
Tothby, Anthony, s Robert Tothby c	23 ,,
Lea, James, s Henry Lea c	25 ,,
Lane, Ann, d George Lane c	25 ,,
Leach, Mary, d Richard Leach c	30 ,,
Atkinson, Susanna, d Gregory Atkinson c	6 Aug.
Smith, John, s John Smith, ironmonger c	8 ,,
Bennett, Robert, s Robert Bennett c	12 ,,
Francis, Elizabeth, d John Francis c	22 ,,
Barron, ——, d William Barron c	10 Sept.
Bradley, John, s John Bradley c	24 ,,
Dales, Esther, d George Dales c	24 ,,
Martindale, Elizabeth, d Christopher Martindale c	15 Oct.
Broughton, Thomas, s Edward Broughton c	15 ,,
Abbott, Ann, d Richard Abbott c	17 ,,
Shotten, Charles, s Charles Shotten c	5 Nov.
Nelsey, William, s John Nelsey c	5 ,,
Wells, Mary, d Thomas Wells, glover c	12 ,,
Hamerton, Thomas, s William Hamerton, c	19 ,,

[Fol. 6a.]

Goake, John, s John Goake c	21 ,,
Pogson, Samuel, s Robert Pogson, deceased c	8 Dec.
Fitch, Elizabeth, d John Fitch, c	8 ,,
Hamerton, Ann, d John Hamerton, woolen draper c	7 ,,
Leedall, Thomas, s John Leedall c	31 ,,
Salmon, Isabell, d George Salmon c	14 Jan.
Parkins, Mary, d Robert Parkins c	14 ,,
Gill, Christopher, s John Gill, of Slouthby c	29 ,,
Soby, Mary, d Thomas Soby c	11 Feb.
Walther, Elizabeth c	11 ,,
Redthorn, John, s Thomas Redthorn c	18 ,,
Beighton, Ann, d William Beighton c	12 Mar.
Leake, Priscilla, d Richard Leake c	17 ,,
Gillam, Ann, d Thomas Gillam c	24 ,,

MARRIAGES, 1643.

Scarborough, Christopher } m Chantrey, Ann	27 April
Beighton, William } m Wells, Ann	6 June
Allis, Robert } m Stevenson, Ann	13 July
Thompson, Thomas } m Bemes, Katherine	8 Aug.
Goulsborrow, William } m Baxter, Bridget	25 Aug.
Watson, William } m Cresby, Gartree	22 Oct.
Mitchell, Robert } m Middleton, Lidia	18 Jan.
Page, Richard } m Tyres, Susanna	8 Feb.
Waterfall, Richard } m Darby, Bridget	15 ,,

[Fol. 6b.]

BURIALS, 1643.

Simpson, John, b	2 April
Mackris, Elizabeth, infant b	2 ,,
Surflet, Robert, b	17 ,,

Baker, Hamlett, adolescence *b*   26 April
Watson, Mary, wife William Watson *b*   28 ,,
Houlteby, Lawrence, adolescence *b*   6 May
Taylor, John, infant *b*   9 ,,
Snoden, Thomas, infant *b*   9 ,,
Martindale, Ann, spinster, *b*   16 ,,
Westeby, Faith, infant *b*   29 ,,
Goulsborrow, William, *b*   3 June
Poutherill. Thomas, infant *b*   5 ,,
Beverley, John, infant *b*   7 ,,
Hall, Ellen, spinster *b*   10 ,,
Taylor, Mary, infant *b*   10 ,,
Pasmore, Katherine, infant *b*   12 ,,
Castledine, Roger, *b*   18 ,,
Burton, Jane, spinster, *b*   10 July
Dickinson, Barbara, spinster *b*   9 ,,
Mitchell, Mary, wife Robert Mitchell *b*   13 ,,
Leach, William, infant *b*   14 ,,
Pogson, Robert *b*   16 ,,
Gibson, Daniel, infant *b*   22 ,,
Lopsey, John, infant *b*   26 ,,
Custledine, Mary, infant *b*   31 ,,
Gibson, John, infant *b*   31 ,,
Smith, Elizabeth *b*   13 Aug.
Atkinson, John, infant *b*   14 ,,
Lawe, Ann, infant *b*   5 Sept.
Francis, Elizabeth, infant *b*   6 ,,
Taylor, Ann, infant *b*   8 ,,
West John, infant *b*   11 ,,
Broughton, Mary, infant *b*   30 ,,
Smith, Roger, of Gainsborough, Quarter-Master-Captaine
     Dickenson Troop *b*   30 ,,
Clark, Susanna infant *b*   3 Oct.
Darby, Robert *b*   12 ,,
Hopton, Sir Ingrom, Knight *b*   13 ,,
Cage, John, a Souldier under Capt. John Moody *b*   15 ,,
Broughton, Thomas *b*   23 ,,
Ruffles, Margaret *b*   2 Nov.
Wells, Margaret, infant *b*   13 ,,
Curtis John, a Souldier *b*   14 ,,
Hamerton, Thomas, infant *b*   27 ,,
Attenell, Alice, *wife* Edward Attenwell *b*   11 Dec.
     [Fol. 7*a*.]
Parish, Margaret, *wife* John Parish *b*   17 ,,
Bocock, Henry *b*   30 ,,
Salmon, Isabell infant *b*   19 Jan.
Skelton, John, infant *b*   20 ,,
Gill, Christopher, infant *b*   5 Feb.
Block, Thomas *b*   13 ,,
Tesle, Margaret, *wife* William Tesle *b*   14 ,,
Stevenson, Margaret *widow* *b*   16 ,,
Kinge, Richard *b*   23 ,,
Lopsey, Thomas *b*   3 Mar.
Haggard, George *b*   10 ,,
Smith, John, Ironmonger *b*   20 ,,
     CHRISTENINGS, 1644.
Brisko, John *s* John Brisko *c*   25 Mar.
Surflet, Robert, *s* Robert Surflet *c*   31 ,,
Coupland, Katherine, *d* George Coupland   6 April

Tayler, John, *s.* Robert Tayler *c*	7 April
Pinder, Thomas, *s.* Peter Pinder *c*	21 ,,
Story, John, *s.* Richard Story *c*	5 May
Burch, Mary, *d.* Thomas Burch *c*	5 ,,
Wright, Thomas, *s.* George Wright *c*	2 June
Throgmorton, Francis, *s.* Ralph Throgmorton, clerk *c*	3 ,,
Urye, Thomas, *s.* Thomas Urye *c*	18 ,,
Holbich, Laurence, *s.* Edmund Holbich *c*	18 ,,
Richardson, Sarah, *d.* Thomas Richardson *c*	20 ,,
Davisen, Mary, *d.* Stephen Davisen *c*	27 July
Pasmor, Christopher, *s.* William Pasmor *c*	11 Aug.
Johnson, Elizabeth, *d.* John Johnson *c*	11 ,,
Mason, John, *s.* Nicholas Mason *c*	16 ,,
Johnson, Elizabeth, *d.* Richard Johnson *c*	19 ,,
Watson, William, *s.* William Watson *c*	15 Sept.
Gersam, Elizabeth, *d.* Hugh Gersam *c*	15 ,,
Lathropp, John, *s.* John Lathropp *c*	18 ,,
Tayler, Ann, *d.* Francis Tayler *c*	22 ,,
White, John, *s.* Charles White *c*	13 Oct.
Page, Thomas, *s.* Richard Page *c*	14 Nov.
Boulton, William, *s.* John Boulton *c*	17 ,,
Portes, George, *s.* George Portes *c*	26 ,,
Tisdale, Susanna, *d.* Robert Tisdale *c*	26 ,,
Looking, William, *s.* John Looking *c*	21 Dec.
Poutherill, William, *s.* Richard Poutherill *c*	21 ,,
Palmer, Mary, *d.* John Palmer *c*	11 Jan.
Crastel, Ann, *d.* Henry Crastel *c*	14 ,,
Tothby, Elizabeth, *d.* Robert Tothby *c*	16 ,,

[Fol. 7b.]

Gibson, Richard, *s.* Robert Gibson *c*	23 ,,
Burton, Grace, *d.* Luke Burton *c*	23 ,,
Francis, Elizabeth, *d.* John Francis *c*	26 ,,
Markby, Ann, *d.* Richard Markby *c*	27 ,,
Leach, Richard, *s.* Richard Leach *c*	12 Feb.
Nichlson, John, *s.* John Nichlson *c*	21 ,,
Westeby, Isabell, *d.* Edward Westeby *c*	23 ,,
West, Mary, *d* John West *c*	24 ,,
Alesby, John, *s.* Robert Alesby *c*	24 ,,
Vinter, Robert, *s.* Richard Vinter *c*	24 ,,
Merriwether, John, spurious bastard child, Elizabeth Merriwether *c*	24 ,,
Smith, Ann, *d* John Smith *c*	24 ,,

MARRIAGES, 1644.

Alesby, Robert Smith, Priscilla } *m*	23 May
Hall, Richard Carrote, Alice } *m*	22 ,,
Franklsh, John Baxter, Mary } *m*	28 ,,
Hastings, Robert Chapman, Ann } *m*	20 Aug.
Bond, William Hamerton, Jane } *m*	22 ,,
Enderby, John Stevenson, Jane } *m*	7 Nov.
Stokes, Thomas Becock, Dorcas } *m*	20 Feb.

[Fol. 8a.]

BURIALS, 1644.

Leake, Priscilla, *b*	25	Mar.
Woodes, ——, *widow b*	3	April
Brisko, John, *b*	5	,,
Markby, Elizabeth, infant *b*	14	,,
Gulsinge, William, adolescence *b*	31	May
Clark, Thomas, infant *b*	17	June
Clark, Christopher, adolescence *b*	31	,,
Holbich, Lawrence, infant *b*	2	July
Grimald, Thomas, *b*	15	,,
Mason, Alice, *wife* Nicholas Mason *b*	16	Aug.
Adam, Hosea, a souldier *b*	19	,,
Grantham, Ann, *widow b*	20	,,
——, a souldier who dyed at widow Druryes, whose name was not known, *b*	20	,,
Knight, John, a souldier *b*	21	,,
Perry, George, a souldier *b*	22	,,
Hall, Joane, *wife* Henry Hall *b*	23	,,
Petch, John, a souldier *b*	23	,,
Goulden, Ralph, a souldier *b*	24	,,
Barret, Tymothie, a souldier *b*	26	,,
——, two souldiers whose names was not knowne *b*	27	,,
Casney, John, a souldier *b*	31	,,
Hanch, Edward, a souldier *b*	4	Sept.
Arnell, Francis, a souldier *b*	5	,,
Skelton, Katherine, *b*	9	,,
Forman, Alice, *widow b*	10	,,
Francis, John, *b*	11	,,
Dalton, George, *b*	11	,,
Spinkes, Mary, *b*	11	,,
Payne, Thomas, a souldier *b*	12	,,
Morgan, Thomas, a souldier *b*	14	,,
Fromwell, John, a souldier *b*	14	,,
Coates, Elizabeth, infant *b*	15	,,
——, a souldier at Captain Marsh's house, whose name was not known *b*	16	,,
Hartley, Thomas, a souldier *b*	16	,,
Walker, Robert, *b*	16	,,
Drury, Elizabeth *b*	16	,,
Holbeach, Ann, *b*	18	,,
Chesbrooke, Robert, *b*	19	,,
Bradley, Margaret, *wife* John Bradley *b*	22	,,
Hattfield, James, a souldier *b*	22	,,
Shaw, Henry, a souldier *b*	24	,,
Goose, William, *b*	24	,,
Brisko, John, *b*	3	Oct.
Nelson, Mary, *wife* Eustace Nelson *b*	11	,,
Pinches, Thomas, infant *b*	13	,,
Sherriff, Bridget, *b*	24	,,
Skelton, James, *b*	27	,,
Knight, Charles, *b*	27	,,
Attinell, Martha, *wife* Christopher Attinell *b*	30	,,

[Fol. 8b].

Ridge, Mary, *wife* Henry Ridge *b*	1	Nov.
Daulton, Ann, *widow b*	3	,,
Garthsted, Ann, *wife* Francis Garthsted *b*	4	,,
Beckworth, Edward, a souldier *b*	6	,,
Castledine, John, adolescence *b*	14	,,

Smith, Eden, widow *b* — 16 Nov.
Smith, Richard, adolescence *b* — 17 „
Passmore, Christopher, infant *b* — 17 „
Boulton, William, infant *b* — 21 „
Hancock, Elizabeth, infant *b* — 21 „
Chappell, Alice, spinster *b* — 24 „
Hogg, Thomas *b* — 2 Dec.
Portes, George *b* — 4 „
Wallesby, Thomas *b* — 9 „
Tisdale, Thomas, infant *b* — 21 „
Soby, Thomas *b* — 7 Jan.
Clay, Grace, wife, Richard Clay *b* — 9 „
Tayler, Ann, widow *b* — 16 „
Benton, Ann, infant *b* — 23 „
Frankis, Elizabeth, wife William Frankis *b* — 25 „
———, ———, a woman who was a stranger *b* — 26 „
Enderby, Jane, wife of John Enderby *b* — 28 Feb.
Barker, Anthony *b* — 5 Mar.
Rowle, William *b* — 18 „
Walker, Ann, spinster *b* — 21 „
Kerk, Judeth, infant *b* — 21 „
Merriwether, John, bastard Childe of Elizabeth Merriwether — 21 „

CHRISTENINGS, 1645.

Gibson, Ann, *d* William Gibson *c* — 13 April
Law, William, *s* George Law *c* — 28 „
Curtis, John, *s* Robert Curtis *c* — 4 May
Wells, Mary, *d* Thomas Wells, glover *c* — 14 „
Beverley, Elizabeth, *d* John Beverley *c* — 20 „
Bococke, John, *s* John Bococke *c* — 25 „
Richardson, Richard, *s* John Richardson *c* — 22 June
Hancock, Steven, *s* Steven Hamock *c* — 24 „
Hall, James, *s* Richard Hall *c* — 26 „
White, John, *s* Thomas White *c* — 3 July
Hamerton, Thomas, *s* Robert Hamerton *c* — 6 „
Brighton, William, *s* William Brighton *c* — 6 „
Clark, Susanna, *d* Thomas Clark *c* — 6 „
Moyser, George, *s* Edward Moyser *c* — 13 „
Rowlhton, Edward, *s* Edward Rowlhton *c* — 8 Aug.

[Fol. 9a.]

Mitchell, Robert, *s* Robert Mitchell *c* — 3 „
Whiting, John, *s* Andrew Whiting *c* — 3 „
Gersam, Isabell, *d* Henry Gersam *c* — 17 „
Wilkinson, William, *s* of Harbert Wilkinson *c* — 7 Sept.
Burch, Isabell, *d* John Burch *c* — 7 „
Bromley, Ellen, *d* John Bromley *c* — 20 „
Helsey, Ellen. *d* John Helsey *c* — 21 „
Blancherd, Frances, *d* John Blancherd *c* — 16 „
Tayler, Thomas, *s* Thomas Tayler *c* — 9 Nov.
Tayler, Isabel, *d* Francis Tayler *c* — 20 „
Pinder, Barbara, *d* Peter Pinder *c* — 23 „
Bitchfield, ———, —, John Bitchfield *c* — 23 „
Nichols, William, *s* Thomas Nichols *c* — 11 Dec.
Fitch, Samuell, *s* John Fitch *c* — 16 „
Enderby, Thomas, *s* Thomas Enderby *c* — 21 „
Martindale, Thomas, *s* Christopher Martindale *c* — 27 „
Holbich, Richard, *s* Edmond Holbich *c* — 31 „
Groome, Georg, *s* Georg Groome *c* — 1 Jan.
Pasmore, Christopher, *s* William Pasmore *c* — 3 Feb.
Smith, Anthony, *s* John Smith *c* — 15 „

Parrish, William, s John Parrish c   15 Feb.
Burch, Thomas, s Thomas Burch c   19 ,,
Parkins, Elizabeth, d Robert Parkins c   22 ,,
Shotten, Elizabeth, d Charles Shotten c   25 ,,

[Fol. 9b.]

MARRIAGES, 1645.

Mason, Nicholas } m
Fetherstone, Margaret }   10 May

Franklsh, William } m
Lawson, Isabel }   12 June

Maultby, William } m
Tirrington, Elizabeth }   24 ,,

Walker, Richard } m
Leman, Ann }   26 ,,

Ridge, Henry } m
Eldridge, Mary }   17 ,,

Rooksby, Richard } m
Bennet, Frances }   13 Nov.

Wardle, John } m
Wright, Mary }   21 Dec.

Wilkinson, Herbert } m
Newman, Frances }   30 ,,

Richardson, James } m
Leary, Elizabeth }   29 Jan.

BURIALS, 1645.

Looking, William, } infants b
Smith, Anne }   27 Mar.
Goulsborrow, Richard, infant, b   20 April
Wright, Thomas, infant b   11 June
Bennett, Robert b   25 ,,
Tayler, John, infant b   19 July
Baxter, Ann, spinster b   25 ,,
Burch, Mary, infant, b   14 Aug.
Richardson, Mary, wife James Richardson b   15 ,,
Richardson, Ann, infant b   18 ,,
Morset, Ellen, spinster b   25 ,,
Goulsborrow, Ann, infant b   2 Sept.
Wilkinson, William. infant b   2 Oct.
Wilkinson, Mary, wife of Herbert Wilkinson b   12 ,,
Surflet, Mary, infant b   20 ,,
Waterfall, Richard, infant   22 ,,
Nelsey, Elizabeth b   6 Nov.
Blancherd, Bryan b   24 ,,
Alesby, John b   28 ,,
Smith, Margaret, widow b   18 Dec.
Bitchfield, William b   19 ,,
Shotten, Charles, infant b   30 ,,
Martindale, Thomas, infant b   1 Jan.
Brisko, Ann, widow b   12 ,,
Parker, Elizabeth, wife of William Parker b   20 ,,
Shotten, Elizabeth, infant b   24 Feb.
Ashton, Richard b   28 ,,

[Fol. 10a.]

CHRISTENINGS, 1646.

Maultby, Isabelle, d William Maultby c   31 Mar.
Dales, Esther, d George Dales c   1 April
Milner, Henry, s Robt. Milner c   5 ,,
Salmon, Edward, s George Salmon   5 ,,
Portes, Elizabeth, d George Portes c   19 ,,

West, John, *s.* Lyonell West *c*   22 April
Bowering, James, *s.* James Bowering *c*   8 May
Franckiss, Hellen, *d.* William Franckiss *c*   10 ,,
Milner, Thomas, *s.* Thomas Milner *c*   17 ,,
Francis, Isabelle *d.* Harmon Francis *c*   1 June
Goulsborrow, Elizabeth, *d.* William Goulsborrow *c*   14 ,,
Crates, Isabelle *d.* Richard Crates *c*   14 ,,
Kerk, Debora, *d.* William Kerk *c*   14 ,,
Mason, Elizabeth, *d.* Nicholas Mason *c*   15 ,,
Page, Richard, *s.* of Richard Page *c*   28 ,,
Tisdale, Jane, *d.* Robert Tisdale *c*   29 ,,
Lovell, Mary, *d* Mr. William Lobell *c*   28 July
Maddison, Edward, the putative bastard of Edward Maddison *c*   30 ,,
Dunn, Ellen, *d.* Stephen Dunn *c*   6 Aug.
Bocock, Richard, *s.* John Bocock *c*   12 ,,
Beighton, Richard, *s.* William Beighton *c*   18 ,,
Walsher, Mary, *d.* John Walsher *c*   6 Sept.
Coates, Susanna, *d.* James Coates *c*   18 ,,
Gillam, Thomas, *s.* Thomas Gillam *c*   21 ,,
Alesby, Elizabeth, *d.* Robert Alesby *c*   18 Oct.
Wilkinson, ——, *s.* Herbert Wilkinson *c*   18 ,,
Woding, Mary, *d.* Philip Woding *c*   2 Nov.
Broughton, Robert, *s.* William Broughton *c*   8 ,,

[Fol. 10*b*.]

Burton, Mary, *d.* Luke Burton *c*   24 ,,
White, Thomas, *s.* Thomas White *c*   29 ,,
Lawe, Elizabeth, *d.* George Lawe *c*   10 Dec.
Richardson, Richard, *s.* James Richardson *c*   13 ,,
Pinder, Thomas, *s.* Peter Pinder *c*   18 ,,
Clarke, Willyam, *s.* Willyam Clarke *c*   18 ,,
Curtis, Thomas bastard childe of Mary Curtis, putative of
     Thomas Smith *c*   29 ,,
Nelsey, Edward, *s.* John Nelsey *c*   10 Jan.
Wells, Ann, *d.* Thomas Wells, glover *c*   17 ,,
Johnson, Robert, *s.* Robert Johnson *c*   17 ,,
Marley, Sarah, *d.* Henry Marley *c*   7 Feb.
Moyser, Mary, *d.* Edward Moyser *c*   7 ,,
Markley, Thomas, *s.* Richard and Ann Markley, butcher
     c 28 Dec. 1646.*
Chapman, John, *s.* John & Mary Chapman, Ironmonger
     c 29 April, 1646.*

[Fol. 11*a*.]

MARRIAGES, 1646.

Nelson, Eustace ⎱ *m*   31 Mar.
Drury, Margaret ⎰

Wright, Gabriel ⎱ *m*   30 April
Wright, Anne ⎰

Parker, Samuel ⎱ *m*   5 July
Skelton, Dorothy ⎰

Pacy, Tymothie ⎱ *m*   8 Oct.
Freston, Elizabeth ⎰

Bromley, John ⎱ *m*   10 Nov.
Ashton, Mary ⎰

Hanson, John ⎱ *m*   17 ,,
Bamber, Ellen ⎰

BURIALS, 1646.

Pinder, Barbara, *b*   2 April

* Omitted in the regular months.

Johnson, James, adolescense *b*	4 April
Lawrence, Edward, adolescense *b*	12 ,,
King, Margaret, widow, *b*	7 May
Peak, Robert, *b*	18 ,,
Simpson, Nazareth, widow, b	24 ,,
Bradley, Benjamine, *b*	18 June
Davison, Mr. William, *b*	17 ,,
Woolby, Mrs. Katherine, widow, *b*	17 ,,
Maddison, Mary, wife George Maddison *b*	2 Aug.
Smith, Willyam, Vintner *b*	4 ,,
Tisdale, Susanna, infant *b*	8 ,,
Tisdale, Jane, infant *b*	15 ,,
Fawcitt, John *b*	13 Oct.
Chappell, Gabriell *b*	6 Nov.
Johnson, James *b*	7 ,,
Hall, Henry *b*	16 ,,
Maddison, George *b*	7 Dec.
Ashton, Alice *b*	11 ,,
Ewing, Robert, a stranger *b*	13 ,,
Lawe, Willyam, infant *b*	29 ,,
Curtis, Thomas, bastard childe of Mary Curtis *b*	15 Jan.
Mason, Elizabeth *b*	5 Feb.

[Fol. 11*b*.]

Pasmore, Christopher, infant *b*	11 Mar.
Markby, George *b*	19 ,,

CHRISTENINGS, 1647.

Crastes, Henry, *s.* Henry Crastes *c*	28 ,,
White Bridget, *d.* Charles White *c*	81 ,,
Parrish, Ann, *d.* John Parrish *c*	2 April
Poutherill, Ann, *d.* Richard Poutherill *c*	4 ,,
Story, Elizabeth, *d.* Richard Story *c*	28 ,,
Coupland, Luke, *s.* George Coupland *c*	9 May
Hancock, Mary, *d.* Stephen Hancock *c*	27 ,,
Wright, Margery, *d.* George Wright *c*	30 ,,
Martindale, Ann, *d.* Christopher Martindale *c*	6 June
Bradley, John, *s.* Richard Bradley *c*	4 July
Vrye, Frances, *d.* Thomas Vrye *c*	6 ,,
Willyman, Mary, *d.* Gilbert Willyman *c*	2 Aug.
Simpson, John, *s.* John Simpson *c*	4 ,,
Leach, Sarah, *d.* Richard Leach *c*	28 ,,
Hanson, Jonothan, *s.* John Hanson *c*	29 ,,
Gunby, Willyam, *s.* Thomas Gunby *c*	16 Sept.
Franckiss, Elizabeth, *d.* William Franckiss *c*	26 ,,
Hamerton, Robert, *s.* Robert Hamerton *c*	3 Oct.
Tothby, Robert, *s.* Robert Tothby *c*	10 ,,
Tayler, Thomas, *s.* Robert Tayler the elder *c*	7 Nov.
Whiting, Elizabeth, *d.* Andrew Whiting *c*	21 ,,
Tayler, Robert, *s.* Robert Tayler the younger *c*	5 Dec.
Bowering, Cicilley, *d.* Jomes Bowering *c*	5 ,,
Hall, Elizabeth, *d.* Richard Hall *c*	18 ,,
Brackenborough, Richard, *s.* Thomas Brackenborough *c*	19 ,,
Dennis, Penelope, *d.* Timothy Dennis *c*	28 ,,
Littlebury, Nathaniell, *s.* Dymock Littlebury *c*	2 Jan.
Markby, Thomas, *s.* Richard Markby *c*	21 ,,

[Fol. 12*a*.]

Maultby, Margaret, *d.* William Maultby *c*	22 ,,
Tayler, John, *s.* Francis Tayler *c*	28 ,,
Coates, Ann, *d.* James Coates *c*	13 Feb.

· Beighton, John *s.* William Beighton *c*   26 Feb.
— Hamerton, Edward, *s.* John Hamerton *c*   16 Mar.

MARRIAGES, 1647.

— Laines, Jeremiah   ⎱ *m*   29 June
· Clapham, Pretazey ⎰
· Ashton, John   ⎱ *m*   18 July
~ Robinson, Sarah ⎰
— Doubty, William ⎱ *m*   16 Nov.
· Hollingsworth, Ann ⎰

[Fol. 12*b*.]

BURIALS, 1647.

~ Wells, Ann *b*	8 April
~ Riley, Richard, tayler *b*	14 ,,
— Martindale, Robert *b*	8 May
— Burch, John *b*	6 ,,
· Gillam, William *b*	15 ,,
~ Houldernes, John *b*	17 ,,
— White, Bridget, infant *b*	25 ,,
— Hancock, Mary, infant *b*	31 ,,
~ Meed, Mary, spinster *b*	15 June
· Surflet, Edward *b*	6 July
— Milner, Bridget, widow *b*	14 ,,
· Westeby, Isabell, infant *b*	24 ,,
~ Francis, Isabel, infant *b*	11 Aug.
· Freston, Elizabeth *b*	19 ,,
· Vinter, Isabel *b*	29 ,,
· Clark, Mary, virginis *b*	4 Sept.
~ Burch, Elizabeth, virginis *b*	16 ,,
— Henman, William, adolescens *b*	17 ,,
· Dawkin, Alice, widow *b*	1 Dec.
~ Whiting, Elizabeth, infant *b*	5 ,,
~ Hamerton, Stephen, adolescens *b*	18 ,,
~ Beighton, William, infant *b*	6 ,,
~ Gunby, William, infant *b*	9 ,,
· Tothby, Thomas *b*	21 ,,
~ Francis, John, senior *b*	28 ,,
· Weisher, Alice, infant *b*	28 ,,
— Pinder, Thomas, adolescens *b*	2 Feb.
— Littlebury, Nathaniel *b*	2 ,,
— Tothby, Ellen, virginis *b*	8 ,,
· Hutchinson, John, adolescens *b*	6 ,,
~ Coates, Ann, infant *b*	16 ,,
~ Wilson, Nicholas *b*	27 ,,
~ Vinter, Edward *b*	2 Mar.
~ Mackris, Isabel, infant *b*	8 ,,
· Peares, Richard, adolescens *b*	21 ,,

[Fol. 13*a*.]

CHRISTENINGS, 1648.

· Holbich, Katherine, *d.* Edmond Holbich *c*	4 April
· Chapman, Elizabeth, *d.* John Chapman *c*	11 ,,
· Mayer, Robert, *s.* Richard Mayer *c*	18 ,,
· Snelland, John, *s.* Christopher Snelland *c*	19 ,,
— Haynes, Margaret, *d.* John Baynes *c*	5 May
· Gersam, Thomas, *s.* Hugh Gersam *c*	7 ,,
— Burch, Faith, *d.* Thomas Burch *c*	9 ,,
· Laines, Thomas, *s.* Jeremiah Laines *c*	14 ,,
Clark, Mary, *d.* Thomas Clark *c*	14 ,,
· Gibson, Ann, *d.* Robert Gibson *c*	21 ,,

-White, Mary, *d.* Charles White *c*   31 May
- Wright, Ann. *d.* Gabriell Wright *c*   18 June
-Vinter, Elizabeth, *d.* Richard Vinter *c*   20 ,,
-Tayler, Mary, *d.* Thomas Tayler *c*   11 July
-Lovell, Thomas, *s.* William Lovell *c*   1 Aug.
-Burton, John, *s.* Luke Burton *c*   9 ,,
-Smith, John, John Smith, tanner *c*   9 ,,
- Lee, Elizabeth, *d.* Henry Lee *c*   11 ,,
- Wells, Susanna, *d.* Thomas Wells *c*   24 ,,
- Boyes, Mark, *s.* Thomas Boyes *c*   27 ,,
-Kerk, Richard, *s.* William Kerk *c*   31 ,,
-Baledam, Margaret, *d.* Edward Baledam *c*   3 Sept.
-Danckes, Elizabeth, *d.* Philip Danckes *c*   3 ,,
-West, Elizabeth, *d.* John West *c*   3 ,,
-Hollingworth, Richard, *s* John Hollingworth *c*   10 ,,
- Vinter, Thomas, *s* Adam Vinter *c*   10 ,,
- Page, Mary, *d* Richard Page *c*   1 Oct.
-Wells, Mary. *d* Thomas Wells deceased *c*   8 ,,
- Barret, Ann, *d* Thomas Barret *c*   22 ,,
- Bromley, Enoch, *s* John Bromley *c*   25 ,,
-Wilkinson, John, *s* Herbert Wilkinson *c*   27 ,,
- Leadan, William, *s* John Leadan *c*   26 Nov.
- Markey, Susanna, *d* Henry Markey *c*   13 Dec.
- Richardson, John, *s* Moses Richardson *c*   17 ,,
-West, Judith, *d* Lionel West *c*   17 ,,
-Hancock, Ann, *d* Stephen Hancock *c*   31 ,,
- Richardson, Elizabeth, *d* James Richardson *c*   31 ,,
- Twentyman, Mary, *d* Robert Twentyman *c*   23 Jan.
- Parrish, Frances, *d* John Parrish *c*   25 ,,
-Poutherill, Francis, *s* Richard Poutherill *c*   25 ,,
- Tisdale, William, *s* Robert Tisdale *c*   22 Feb.
- Gillam, Richard, *s.* Thomas Gillam *c*   25 ,,
- Welsher, Alice, *d* John Welsher *c*   25 ,,

[Fol. 13b.]

- Bowering, Hugh, *s* James Bowering *c*   4 Mar.
-Fitch, Joshua, *s* John Fitch *c*   15 ,,
- Martin, Rachel, *d* Charles Martin *c*   15 ,,
- Goulsborrow, Alice, *d* William Goulsborrow *c*   18 ,,

MARRIAGES, 1648.

-Hassell, Thomas }
-Johnson, Margaret } *m*   4 May
-Johnson, Roger }
-Richardson, Grace } *m*   16 ,,
-Foster, Henry }
-Hamerton, Elizabeth } *m*   1 June
-Wright, William }
-Baxter, Magdalen } *m*   20 July
-Pinder, Peter }
-Bowden, Sussanna } *m*   31 Aug.
- Bitchfield, John }
——, Margaret } *m* Lisence   2 Jan.
- Hamerton, Thomas }
-Tayler, Mary } *m*   13 Feb.
- Garthside, John }
- Eldrige, Christian } *m*   26 Mar.

[Fol. 14a.]

BURIALS, 1648.
- Wells, Thomas, tanner *b*   6 April
- Wilson, Mary, a stranger *b*   9 ,,

Nichols, William, infant *b*	12 April
Parkins, Gyles, *b*	21 ,,
Stokes, Margaret, *b*	21 ,,
Snelland, John, infant *b*	27 ,,
Gersam, Thomas, infant *b*	12 May
Tayler, Thomas, infant *b*	21 ,,
Pinder, Elizabeth, *b*	22 ,,
Salmon, John, *b*	28 ,,
Duffin, Magdalen, spinster *b*	27 ,,
Mayer, Robert, infant *b*	8 June
Grimald, Elizabeth, *b*	16 ,,
Vinter, Elizabeth, infant *b*	20 ,,
White, Mary, infant *b*	28 ,,
Morley, Susanna, *b*	29 ,,
Simpson, Elizabeth, infant *b*	14 July
Atkinson, Rosamond, *b*	24 ,,
Atkinson, Thomas, her husband *b*	29 ,,
Lill, Susanna, spinster *b*	14 Aug.
Smith, Alice, widow *b*	29 Sept.
Bitchfield, Margaret, *b*	14 Oct.
Sillitoe, Henry, *b*	21 ,,
Pogson, William, *b*	5 Dec.
Smith, Colesticia, wife Robert Smith *b*	5 ,,
Lyall, Susanna, wife Thomas Lyall *b*	15 ,,
Frest, Elizabeth, wife Thomas Frest *b*	16 ,,
Richardson, John, infant *b*	21 ,,
Hollingworth, Symon, *b*	22 ,,
Nelson, Margaret, wife England Nelson *b*	27 ,,
Lettin, Elizabeth, widow *b*	29 ,,
West, Elizabeth, infant *b*	2 Jan.
Wright, Ann, infant *b*	11 ,,
Wells, Margaret, *b*	21 ,,
Sheriffe, William, *b*	18 Feb.
Watson, John, *b*	25 ,,
Sheriffe, Margaret, widow *b*	28 ,,
Poutherill, Francis, infant *b*	25 ,,
Laines, Thomas, *b*	22 Mar.
Tisdale, Margaret, wife Robert Tisdale *b*	28 ,,

[Fol. 14*b*.]

CHRISTENINGS, 1649.

Foster, Sarah, *d* Henry Foster *c*	29 Mar.
Butler, Thomas, *s* Thomas Butler, Edlington *c*	1 April
Clark, Thomas. *s* Henry Clark *c*	8 ,,
Mayer, Anne, *d* Richard Mayer *c*	8 May
Gibson, Marmaduke, *s* William Gibson *c*	6 ,,
Dawson, John, *s* Thomas Dawson *c*	20 ,,
Franks, Peter, *s* William Franks *c*	20 ,,
Pinder, Joyes, *d* Peter Pinder *c*	10 June
Randes, Katheren, *d* Mr. Edmond Randes *c*	16 ,,
Coates, Elizabeth, *d* James Coates *alias* Deane *c*	1 July
Vrye, Kathren, *d* Thomas Vrye *c*	5 ,,
Crastes, John, *s* Henry Crastes *c*	8 ,,
Hamerton, Mary, *d* Samuel Hamerton *c*	8 ,,
Wright, Frances, *d* Gabriell Wright *c*	8 ,,
Enderby, Jonah, *s* Thomas Enderby *c*	2 Aug.
Simpson, Richard, *s* John Simpson *c*	6 ,,
Leach, Alice, *d* Richard Leach *c*	7 ,,
Moyser, Elizabeth, *d* Edward Moyser *c*	29 Sept.
Clarke, Christopher, *s* Francis Clarke *c*	2 Oct.

Bocock, Edward, s John Bocock c   8 Oct.
Bitchfield, Thomas, s John Bitchfield c   4 ,,
Snoden, Thomas, s Rutland Snoden c   16 ,,
Wrightson, Mary, d Edward Wrightson c   18 Nov.
Davison, Ann, d Setphen Davison c   18 ,,
Bradley, Stephen, s Richard Bradley c   81 Dec.
Chapman, Joseph, s John Chapman c   81 ,,
[Fol. 15a.]
Laines, Jeremiah, s Jeremiah Laines c   18 Jan.
Tayler, Elizabeth, d Robert Tayler c   18 ,,
Hutchinson, Robert, s John Hutchinson c   81 ,,
Wright, Frances, d George Wright c   10 Feb.
West, Elizabeth, d John West c   10 ,,
Lawrence, Hannah, d Robert Lawrence c   14 ,,
Lawe, Faith, d Mr. Obadiah Lawe c   17 ,,
Pell, Katherine, d James Pell c   19 ,,
Hanson, Mary, d John Hanson   10 Jul.*
[Fol. 15b.]

BURIALS, 1649.

Butler, Thomas, infant b   18 April
Patchett, Robert b   12 June
Randes, Katherine, infant b   18 ,,
Vrye, Katheren, infant b   11 July
Hall, Elizabeth, infant b   29 ,,
Coates, Elizabeth, infant b   14 Aug.
Enderby, Jonah, infant b   2 Sept.
Crastes, John, infant b   18 ,,
Croston, Ann b   28 ,,
Pibus, Merrivall b   14 Oct.
Tysdale, William, infant b   29 ,,
Kent, Sarah Virginis b   18 Nov.
Foster, Sarah, infant b   14 ,,
Mitchell, Robert b   28 ,,
Burch, Faith, d Thomas Burch b   5 Jan.
Cooper, Francis, of Minting b   12 ,,
Hanson, Elizabeth, wife of William Hanson b   29 ,,
Parrish, John, s John Parrish b   10 Mar.
[Fol. 16a.]

MARRIAGES, 1649.

Freston, Richard } m   8 May
Hall, Deborah

Parker, Thomas } m   15 Nov.
Scott, Alice

CHRISTENINGS, 1650.

Lovell, Elizabeth, d William Lovell c   4 April
Freston, Katherine, d Richard Freston c   7 ,,
Foster, Nathaniel, s Henry Foster c   14 ,,
Pacey, Joseph, s Timothy Pacey c   19 May
Goode, Mary, d John Goode c   21 ,,
Bowering, Jane, d James Bowering c   8 June
Francis, Elizabeth, d John Francis c   6 ,,
Tayler, Grace, d Francis Tayler c   9 ,,
Turner, Robert, s David Turner c   10 ,,
Leadall, Hugh, s John Leadall c   28 ,,
Smith, Mary, d Robert Smith c   80 ,,
White, William c   15 July
Bradley, Henry, s Jos. Bradley c   11 Aug.

---

* Omitted in month of July.

Hailbey, Ann, *d* William Hailbey *c*   11 Aug.
Nelsey, Thomas, *s* John Nelsey *c*   25   ,,
Plumpton, Jane, *d* George Plumpton *c*   25   ,,
Hamerton, Mary, *d* Robert Hamerton *c*   1 Sept.
Wright, Peter, *s* Thomas Wright *c*   8   ,,
Coates, Ann, *d* James Coates *c*   8   ,,
Beighton, William, *s* William Beighton *c*   22   ,,
Burton, Margaret, *d* Luke Burton *c*   22   ,,

[Fol. 16*b*.]

Maidens, Ann, *d* Edward Maidens *c*   27 Oct.
Gersame, Francis, *s* Hugh Gersame *c*   8 Nov.
Burch, Mary, *d* William Burch *c*   10   ,,
Locking, Ellen, *d* John Locking *c*   10   ,,
Page, Nicholas, *s* Richard Page *c*   15   ,,
Crastes, Thomas, *s* Henry Crastes *c*   17   ,,
Enderby, William, *s* William Enderby *c*   19   ,,
Holbich, Prudence, *d* Edmond Holbich *c*   24   ,,
Twentyman, John, *s* Robert Twentyman *c*   24   ,,
Maultby, William, *s* William Maultby *c*   1 Dec.
Parrish, Sarah, *d* John Parrish *c*   11   ,,
Harrisse, Lettis, *d* Hugh Harrisse *c*   15   ,,
Parker, William, *s* Thomas Parker *c*   5 Jan.
Gersame, Edward, *s* Henry Gersame *c*   19   ,,
Davison, Thomas, *s* Thomas Davison *c*   19   ,,
Frankish, John, *s* William Frankish *c*   19   ,,
Smith, Ann, *d* John Smith, tanner *c*   9 Feb.
Hollingworth, Susanna, *d* Richard Hollingworth *c*   11   ,,
Dunn, Mary, *d* Philip Dunn *c*   16   ,,
Hamerton, Elizabeth, *d* Samuel Hamerton *c*   14 Mar.
Richardson, Thomas, *s* James Richardson *c*   16   ,,

MARRIAGES, 1650.

Woodthorp, Thomas }
Stubbs, Margaret } *m*   4 July
Franks, Harmon   }
Salmon, Susannah } *m*   1 Oct.
Clark, Richard   }
Richardson, Grace } *m*   1 Nov.

[Fol. 17*a*.]

BURIALS, 1650.

Wilson, Ann, widow *b*   27 April
Stokes, Nicholas *b*   30   ,,
Turner, Robert, infant *b*   30 June
Welsher, Alice, infant *b*   1 July
Francis, Alice, wife Hermon Francis *b*   3   ,,
Vinter, Thomas, infant *b*   10   ,,
Tayler, Mary, infant *b*   15   ,,
Daunse, George, infant *b*   16   ,,
White, William, infant *b*   17   ,,
Henday, Margaret, infant *b*   19   ,,
Hawley, Augten *b*   21   ,,
Rookaby, Richard *b*   30   ,,
Mereweather, Margaret *b*   7 Aug.
White, Katherine, wife Thomas White *b*   19   ,,
Robson, Alice, widow *b*   10 Sept.
Broughton, Mary *b*   22   ,,
Nelsey, John *b*   23   ,,
Chapman, Joseph, infant *b*   5 Oct.
Coates, Ann, infant *b*   11   ,,
Yates, Richard *b*   26   ,,

- Dennys, Elizabeth, wife Charles Dennys *b* ... 4 Nov.
- Lusby, Charles *b* ... 14 ,,
- Page, Nicholas *b* ... 28 ,,
- Porter, Robert *b* ... 24 ,,
- Howgrave, Alice *b* ... 27 ,,
- Whiting, Susanna *b* ... 27 ,,
- Skeene, Ann, a stranger *b* ... 9 Dec.
- Francis, Esther, wife John Francis *b* ... 26 ,,
- Smith, Mary, infant *b* ... 29 ,,
- Francks, Peter, infant *b* ... 30 ,,
- Parrish, Sarah, infant *b* ... 2 Jan.
- King, Faith, widow *b* ... 4 ,,
- Markby, Richard, Junior *b* ... 15 ,,
- Maidens, Ann, infant *b* ... 20 ,,

[Fol. 17*b*.]

CHRISTENINGS, 1651.
- Bromley, Thomas, *s* John Bromley *c* ... 31 Mar.
- Wilkinson, Ann, *d* Herbert Wilkinson, mercer *c* ... 31 ,,
- Chapman, Jonathon, *s* John Chapman *c* ... 9 April
- Pell, John, *s* James Pell *c* ... 10 ,,
- Foster, Elizabeth, *d* Henry Foster *c* ... 27 ,,
- Pinder, Frances, *d* Peter Pinder *c* ... 11 May
- Simpson, Robert, *s* John Simpson *c* ... 18 ,,
- Howe, Obadiah, *s* Mr. Obadiah Howe *c* ... 26 ,,
- Garthside, Elizabeth, *d* John Garthside *c* ... 12 June
- Tothby, Mary, *d* Robert Tothby *c* ... 22 ,,
- Tayler, Jane, *d* Thomas Tayler *c* ... 22 ,,
- Simpson, Elizabeth, *d* William Simpson *c* ... 27 July
- Woodthorpe, Ann, *d* Thomas Woodthorpe *c* ... 3 Aug.
- Clark, Stephen, *s* Henry Clark *c* ... 10 ,,
- Kerk, Francis, *s* William Kerk *c* ... 7 Sept.
- West, Elizabeth, *d* Lyonell West *c* ... 14 ,,
- Tayler, Edward, *s* Robert Tayler *c* ... 29 Oct.
- Hamerton, Joseph, *s* Robert Hamerton, glover *c* ... 3 Nov.
- Vrye, Katherine, *d* Thomas Vrye *c* ... 6 ,,
- Page, Ann, *d* Richard Page *c* ... 7 ,,
- Bocock, Ellen, *d* John Bocock *c* ... 9 ,,
- Hutchinson, Elizabeth, *d* John Hutchinson *c* ... 11 ,,
- Johnson, Elizabeth, *d* Martin Johnson *c* ... 18 ,,
- Brakenborrow, William, *s* Thomas Brakenborrow *c* ... 14 Dec.
- Burton, Elizabeth, *d* Luke Burton *c* ... 23 ,,
- Cooper, Mary, *d* Austine Cooper *c* ... 23 ,,
- Leadall, Joseph, *s* John Leadall *c* ... 1 Jan.
- Wright, John, *s* Gabriell Wright *c* ... 4 ,,
- Bitchfield, William, *s* John Bitchfield *c* ... 4 ,,
- Lovell, Faith, *d* Mr. William Lovell *c* ... 6 ,,
- Barnes, Mary, *d* John Barnes *c* ... 15 ,,
- Clarke, Faith, *d* Francis Clarke *c* ... 24 ,,

[Fol. 18*a*.]

- Johnson, Alice, *d* John Johnson *c* ... 25 ,,
- Handes, Thomas, *s* Thomas Handes *c* ... 4 Feb.
- Pasmore, Elizabeth, *d* William Pasmore *c* ... 4 ,,
- Parish, John, *s* John Parish *c* ... 5 ,,
- Mayer, Tabitha, *d* Thomas Mayer *c* ... 24 ,,
- Tayler, Thomas, *s* Francis Tayler *c* ... 14 ,,

MARRIAGES, 1651.
- Bennett, Thomas }
- Attenell, Joane } *m* ... 18 Sept.

Harding, John } *m*
Warde, Mary }   12 Feb.

[Fol. 18*b*.]

BURIALS, 1651.

Snoden, Mrs. Abigail,* widow *b*   21 April
Chapman, Jonathan, infant *b*   25 ,,
Blansherd, Thomas *b*   28 ,,
Fawcitt, Ann, widow *b*   1 May
Locking, Ellen, infant *b*   10 ,,
Foster, Elizabeth, infant *b*   27 ,,
Tayler, Elizabeth, infant *b*   11 June
Garthside, Elizabeth, infant *b*   14 ,,
Attewell, Edward *b*   23 ,,
Hogg, Jane, widow *b*   25 ,,
Hamerton, Mary, wife Samuell Hamerton *b*   14 July
Tayler, Jane, infant *b*   20 ,,
Baledam, Elizabeth, wife Edward Baledam *b*   31 Aug.
Davison, Jeremiah *b*   4 Sept.
West, Lionell *b*   26 ,,
West, Ann, widow *b*   3 ,,
Broughton, Anne, wife Edward Broughton *b*   11 ,,
Harrison, Nicholas *b*   21 Jan.
Drury, Jane, wife Nicholas Drury *b*   8 Feb.
Nelsey, Thomas, infant *b*   13 ,,
Maultby, William *b*   21 ,,
Watson, Gartrett, wife William Watson, labourer *b*   5 May
Tayler, Thomas, infant *b*   16 Mar.

CHRISTENINGS, 1652.

Davison, Thomas, *s* Steven Davison *c*   26 Mar.
Mackris, Ellen, *d* Christopher Mackris *c*   28 ,,
Garthside, Ann, *d* John Garthside *c*   29 ,,
Harrisse, John, *s* Hugh Harrisse *c*   4 April
Laines, Elizabeth, *d* Jeremie Lames *c*   7 ,,
Redthorne, George, *s* Thomas Redthorne *c*   80 May
Foster, Ann, *d* Henry Foster *c*   9 June
Martindale, Christopher, *s* of Christopher Martindale *c*   30 ,,
Leach, William, *s* Richard Leach, woollen draper *c* 29 Sept.

[Fol. 19*a*.]

Bradley, Henry, *s* Richard Bradley *c*   18 July
Cotes, Steven, *s* James Cotes *c*   19 ,,
Tayler, Robert, *s* Thomas Tayler *c*   25 ,,
Twentyman, Erances, *d* Robert Twentyman *c*   11 Aug.
Wells, John, *s* Thomas Wells, glover *c*   16 Sept.
Maydens, Margrett, *d* Edward Maydens *c*   21 Oct.
Goode, Margery, *d* John Goode *c*   28 ,,
Beighton, Elizabeth, *d* William Beighton *c*   28 ,,
Simpson, William, *s* William Simpson *c*   28 Nov.
Hamerton, Martha, *d* John Hamerton *c*   7 Dec.
Hollingworth, William, *s* John Hollingworth *c*   8 ,,
Page, Mary, *d* Thomas Page *c*   10 Feb.
Maddison, Mary, *d* William Maddison *c*   6 Mar.
Gillam, John, *s* Thomas Gillam *c*   13 ,,
How, Elizabeth, *d* Mr. Obadiah How *c*   20 ,,

[Fol. 19*b*.]

MARRIAGES, 1652.

Milner, Joseph } *m*
Keale, Ellen   }   22 May

---

* Relict of Robert Snoden, Bishop of Carlisle, 1616-1621.

Watson, William }
Bosse, Mary } *m*   3 Aug.

Shotten, Edward }
Drury, Susanna } *m*   3 Aug.

Batty, Francis }
Evers, Elizabeth } *m*   17 „

Tinker, Thomas }
Wells, Ann } *m*   23 „

BURIALS, 1652.
Cooke, Thomas, miller *b*   27 Mar.
Garthside, Katherine *b*   1 April
Garthside, Ann, infant *b*   6 „
Garthside, John, adolescence *b*   21 May
Foster, Elizabeth, wife Henry Foster *b*   8 June
Lamb, Joane, wife Edward Lamb *b*   27 „
Markby, Richard, infant *b*   29 „
Parrish, John, infant *b*   2 July
Lawrence, Job, infant *b*   10 „
Perkins, Elizabeth, *b*   31 „
Coates, Stephen, infant *b*   8 Aug.
Garthside, Thomas, adolescence *b*   18 „
Burton, Mary, infant *b*   4 Sept.
Laines, Elizabeth, widow *b*   18 „
Hamerton, John, the elder *b*   24 Sept.
Thomas, Thompson *b*   17 Oct.
Huggard, Frances, widow *b*   17 „
Peares, Anne, wife Ricyard Peares *b*   21 „
Cooke, Alice *b*   21 „
Drury, Nicholas *b*   31 „
Dowse, William, *s* William Dowse, of Poolam *b*   14 Nov.
Tayler, Richard *b*   5 Dec.
Goisborrow, Ellen *b*   12 „
Clarke, Katherine *b*   12 „
Burch, Elizabeth, wife Thomas Burch *b*   27 „
Dennys, Charles, woolen draper *b*   29 „
Kerke, Mary, wife Clement Kerke *b*   15 Jan.
Tessie, William *b*   28 „

[Fol. 20*a*.]

CHRISTENINGS, 1653.
Sherwin, Mary, *d* Robert Sherwin *c*   6 April
Wilkinson, Thomas, *s* Herbert Wilkinson *c*   17 „
Richardson, Anne, *d* Mayses Richardson *c*   17 „
Freston, Anne, *d* Richard Freston *c*   26 June
Crastes, Mary, *d* Henry Crastes *c*   7 Aug.
Burton, Mary, *d* Luke Burton *c*   13 Sept.
Milner, Elizabeth, *d* Robert Milner *c*   18 „
Hutchinson, Frances, *d* John Hutchinson, yeoman, and
    Elizabeth his wife, borne the 27th of September, 1653 *c*   11 Oct.
Hamerton, Ann, *d* Robert Hamerton, glover, and Ann his
    wife, borne the 28th of September, 1653 *c*   2 „
Markby, Richard, *s* Richard Markby, butcher, and Ann his wife 12 June

[Fol. 20*b*. Blank.]
[Fol. 21*a*.]

MARRIAGES, 1653.
Fowler, Robert }
Ray, Mary } *m*   5 May

Kerklard, John }
Gibson, Martha } *m*   17 „

Peares, Richard
Simpson, Susanna } m   4 Aug.

Peares, Ezekiell
Barron, Ann } m   15 Sept.

BURIALS, 1653.

Hudson, Elizabeth, spinster *b*   30 Mar.
Peake, Thomas *b*   19 June
Sparke, Vincent *b*   19 ,,
Wright, John, infant *b*   27 ,,
Francis, Susanna, wife Hermon Francis *b*   2 Aug.
Moyzer, Julian, wife Edward Moyzer *b*   3 ,,
Pinder, Peter *b*   5 ,,
Golsborrow, Alice, infant *b*   12 ,,
Peares, Ann, wife Ensoby Peares *b*   27 ,,
Foster, John, of Great Steeping *b*   30 ,,
Goke, John, *b*   4 Sept.
Howell, Bartholomew *b*   23 ,,

GENTLE READER since this Act of Parlement
came forth for Regestering of all Marriages
Births and Burialls, you will finde divers disorders
Regestered, by reason, I had noe intelligence nor
came to my view, but neglected by Parents and
other friends till others were Regestered before
them, I therefore desire you would give me leave
to excuse my self wherin I am not Guilty,
hopeing that when it is lookt upon with an
impartill eye, you will not Condemne him whoe will ever
Remain yo\u02b3 Servant in the Lord
— JOHN HARDING
Parrish Regester.

[Fol. 21*b*.]

A true Regester of all the Births Marriages and Burialls within the
parish of Horncastle since the 29th day of September, 1653, according
to an Act of Parliam\u1d57 in that case made and provided kept by John
Harding elected Regester by the Inhabitants thereof and approved
and sworne by Richard Bryan Esquire one of the Justices of the
Peace for the s\u1d48 psh. according to the said Act.

Etherington, Ann, *d* John and Joane Etherington, tanner,
   borne 8 Oct., 1653 *c*   17 Oct.
Smith, John, *s* John Smith, Ironmonger, borne 7 Oct. *c*   6 Nov.
Mayer, Edward, *s* Thomas and Dorcas Mayer, barber, borne
   12 Oct. *c*   17 Oct.
Vinter, Mattathias, *d* Adam and Jane Vinter, laborer, borne
   31 Oct. *c*   6 Nov.
White, Stephen, *s* Thomas and Susanna, weaver, borne 5 Nov. *c*   9 ,,
Graves, Lawrence, *s* Ralph Graves, sadler, borne 14 Oct. *c*   25 Oct.
Parker, Robert, *s* Thomas and Alice Parker, glover, borne 26
   Nov. *c*   27 Nov.
Tayler, George, *s* Francis and Grace Tayler, glover, borne 19
   Nov. *c*   20 ,,
Hill, Charles, *s* Gabriell and Ann Hill, borne 2 Dec. *c*   6 Dec.
Dankes, Ellen, *d* Phillip Dankes, borne 16 Jan. *c*   22 Jan.
Page, John, *s* Richard and Susanna Page, currier, borne 28
   Jan. *c*   1 Feb.
Simpson, Thomas, *s* John Simpson, borne 1 Feb. *c*   5 ,,

[Fol. 22*a*.]

Batty, Ann, *d* Francis and Elizabeth Batty, barbour, borne 25
   Jan. *c*   6 ,,

Clarke, Ann, *d* Henry Clarke, labourer, borne 2 Feb. *c*	12 Feb.
Wright, Mary, *d* Gabriell and Ann Wright, glover, borne 7 Feb. *c*	12 ,,
Hamerton, John, *s* John Hamerton, the younger, tanner, borne 25 Feb. *c*	26 ,,
Fowler, Robert, *s* Robert and Mary Fowler, glover, borne 27 Feb. *c*	6 Mar.
Leach, John, *s* Richard and Sarah Leach, woolen draper, borne 28 Feb. *c*	5 ,,
Harris, Rebecca, *d* Hugh and Alice Harris, labourer, borne 19 Feb. *c*	19 ,,

BIRTHS AND CHRISTENINGS, 1654.

Bocock, John, *s* John and Mary Bocock, laborer, borne 4 April *c*	9 April
Howgrave, Elizabeth, *d* Alexander and Mary Howgrave, borne 7 April *c*	20 ,,
Alesby, Robert, *s* Robert and Priscilla Alesby, tayler, boone 11 April *c*	13 ,,
Huddlestone, Frances, *d* Hamlett and Margarett Huddlestone shoemaker, borne 26 March *c*	16 ,,
Plumpton, Job, *s* George and —— Plumpton, borne 17 April *c*	23 ,,
Woodthorp, Elizabeth, *d* Thomas and Margaret Woodthorp, borne 13 April *c*	23 ,,
Watson, Jane, *d* William and Mary Watson, labourer, borne 16 April *c*	23 ,,
Simpson, Alice, *d* William and Alice Simpson, borne 2 April *c*	30 ,,

[Fol. 22b.]

Hollingworth, Mary, *d* Richard and Susanna Hollingworth, borne 24 April *c*	7 May
Shotten, Charles, *s* Edward and Susanna Shotten, borne 11 May *c*	15 ,,
Hindes, John, *s* Thomas and Frances Hyndes, labourer, borne 29 May *c*	4 June
Burwell, Thomas, *s* James Burwell, shooemaker, borne 23 June *c*	28 ,,
Greene, James, *s* Robert and Sarah Greene, labourer, borne 1 July *c*	2 July
Markby, Richard, *s* Richard and Ann Markby, butcher, borne 13 June *c*	23 June
West, John, *s* John and Margaret West, shoemaker, borne 24 July *c*	24 July
Parrish, John, *s* John and Hellen Parrish, taylor, borne 30 July *c*	30 ,,
Maitland,* Peregrine, *s* Patrick and Isabell Maitland, clerke, borne 23 May *c*	29 May
Dawson, William } *s* and *d* Thomas and Magdalen Dawson, Dawson, Judeth } labourer, borne 2 Sept. *c*	3 Sept.
Chapman, Benjamine, *s* John and Mary Chapman, ironmonger, borne 5 Sept.	
Burton, Mary, *d* Luke and Mary Burton, woollen draper, borne Sept. *c*	,,
Laines, Margaret, *d* Jeremiah Laines, butcher, borne 28 Sept. *c*	2 Oct.
Fisher, Alice, *d* Christopher Fisher, white smith, borne 11 Oct. *c*	17 ,,
Gentle, Susan, *d* Benjamine Gentle, labourer, borne 12 Nov. *c*	16 Nov.
Coop, Jane, *d* Austine Coop, weaver, borne 10 Nov. *c*	19 ,,

[Fol. 23a.]

Tinker, Lidya, *d* Thomas and Ann Tinker, tayler, borne 20 Nov. *c*	3 Dec.

* Note on margin—"omitted of the month of May."

—Warde, Joseph, *s* William Warde *c*	8 Jan.
—Smith,* William, *s* John and Elizabeth Smith, tanner, borne 18 Aug. *c*	4 Oct.
Johnson, Anne, *d* John and Margaret Johnson, borne 21 Jan. *c*	28 Jan.
Tothby, Robert, *s* Robert Tothby, tanner, borne 15 Jan. *c*	28 ,,
Webster, John, *s* Henry and Mary Webster, shoemaker, borne 1 Feb. *c*	5 Feb.
—Wilkinson, William, *s* Herbert and Frances Wilkinson, labourer, borne 17 Jan. *c*	5 ,,
Peares, Ellen, *d* Richard and Susanna Peares, borne 8 Feb. *c*	15 ,,
Neheux, Francis, *s* James and Ann Neheux, lym'er, borne 11 Jan. *c*	20 Feb.
Francis, Alice, *d* Hermon and Ann Francis, glover, borne 26 Feb. *c*	6 Mar.
Maidens, Edmund, *s* Edmund and Margaret Maidens, tayler, borne 9 Jan. *c*	Jan.
—Maultby, Alice, *d* William and Elizabeth Maultby, borne 9 March *c*	18 Mar.
Goode, James, *s* John and Margery Goode, tayler, borne 6 March *c*	18 ,,
—Burch, Samuell, *s* Thomas and Margaret Burch, tanner, borne 25 Feb. *c*	22 ,,
Cater, John, *s* Richard and Mary Cater, chandler, borne 10 March *c*	20 ,,
—Frankis, Ann, *d* William and Isabell Frankis, shoemaker, borne 27 Dec. *c*	4 Jan.
Fowler, Ann, *d* Robert Fowler, borne 21 March, 1654 *c*	25 Mar. 1655.
—Maitland, John, *s* Patrick Maitland, clerk, borne 19 Feb., 1655 *c*	12 Mar.

[Fol. 23b.]

MARRIAGES SINCE 1653.

—Francis, Hermon } *m* Cooke, Ann }	5 Dec.
—Moyser, Edward } *m* Hall, Alice }	12 Jan.
—Burch, Thomas } *m* Tayler, Margaret }	2 May
—Tayler, Lawrence } *m* Peares, Anne }	9 ,,
—Graves, Lawrence } *m* Browne, Phoebe }	30 ,,
Dymok, Mr. Edward } *m* Snoden, Mrs. Abigail }	17 July
Peares, Eustoby } *m* Kerk, Mary }	17 ,,
—Peares, John } *m* Vinter, Bridget }	27 ,,

The contract of Matrimony betweene Mr. Edw. Dymok and Mrs. Abigail Snowden were published the 25th June, the 2th of July, and the 9th July, 1654.

[Fol. 24a.]

BURIALS SINCE MICHAEL., 1653.

Price, Charles, haberdasher *b*	4 Oct.
Graves, Anne, wife Lawrence Graves *b*	4 ,,
Burton, Mary, infant *d* Luke Burton, woolen draper *b*	9 ,,
Crastes, Mary, *d* Henry Crastes, cutler *b*	14 ,,

* Note on margin—"omitted in the month of Aug."

Gibson, Mary, wife Robert Gibson, butcher *b*   25 Oct
Dancks, Mary, infant *d* Philip Dancks, bricklayer *b*   9 Nov.
Tayler, Margaret, wife Laurance Tayler, labourer, *b*   15 „
Blowe, Elizabeth, spinster *b*   30 „
Beverley, Elizabeth, *d* John Beverley *b*   3 Dec.
Hall, Richard, labourer *b*   8 „
Blansherd, Frances, *d* John Blansherd *b*   19 „
Peake, Alice, widdow *b*   20 „
Gerstame, Henry, labourer *b*   25 „
Mitchell, Lidya, widdow *b*   25 „
Vinter, Mattathias, *d* Adam Vinter, labourer *b*   23 „
Vinter, Jane, wife Adam Vinter *b*   24 „
Deane, Ann, *als.* Cotes, widdow *b*   30 Jan.
Maultby, Robert, *s* William Maultby *b*   31 „
Freston, Thomas, butcher *b*   3 Feb.
Hill, Bartholomew, *s* Charles Hill *b*   5 „
Walsh, Ann, *d* Robert Walsh *b*   6 „
Bose, ———, widdow, ——— *b*   15 „
Wright, Mary, *d* Gabriell Wright *b*   15 „
Hamerton, John, *s* John Hamerton the younger, tanner *b*   13 Mar.

[Fol. 24*b*.]

BURIALS, 1654.

Temple, Ann, spinster, *d* ——- Temple of Horsington *b*   15 „
Burch, Isabell, *d* Ellen Burch, widdow *b*   29 „
Bingham, John, weaver and a stranger *b*   12 April
Alesby, Robert, infant *b*   10 May
Boulton, John, Shoomaker *b*   7 June
Simpson, Thomas, infant *b*   16 „
Snoden, Nathaniell, infant *b*   20 „
Burwell, James, infant *b*   28 „
Hutchinson, Mary, Spinster *b*   11 July
Davison, Ann, *d* Stephen Davison *b*   18 „
West, Margaret, wife John West, shoomaker *b*   27 „
Mayer, Thomas, barber *b*   4 Aug.
Hamerton, Mary, widdow *b*   14 „
Lambe, Edward *b*   4 Sept.
Dawson, William, *s* Thomas and Magdalen Dawson, labourer *c*   13 „
Bell, Margaret, *d* John Bell, taylor *b*   23 „
Parrish, John, *s* John Parrish *b*   12 Oct.
Clapham, Edmund, baker *b*   1 Nov.
Simpson, Richard, *s* John Simpson, labourer *b*   11 „
Goode, Alice, *d* John Goode, taylor *b*   18 „
Hendrey, Isabell, wife Edward Hendrey *b*   26 „
Bonner, Robert, a young man *b*   7 Dec.
Smith, Annie, *d* John Smith, tanner *b*   16 „
Harris, John, *s* Hugh Harris, labourer *b*   22 Jan.
Burch, Faith, *d* Ellen Burch, widdow *b*   24 „
Harding, Richard, *s* John Harding *b*   18 Mar.
    1655
Laines, Jeremiah *b*   8 April
Frankiss, William, shoemaker *b*   18 „
Lawrence, Robert, haberdasher *b*   22 „

[Fol. 25*a*.]

Broughton, William, glover *b*   25 „
Burton, Sarah, *d* Luke Burton, woollen draper *b*   16 May
Newman, William, laborer *b*   21 „
Ridg, Henry, blacksmith *b*   1 June
Franks, Ann, infant *b*   1 „

Broughton, Isabel, widow *b*   4 June
Portes, William, *s* George Portes *b*   10 ,,
Laines, John, *s* William Laines, taylor *b*   8 July
Simpson, Ann, wife John Simpson, laborer *b*   6 ,,
Garthside, William, *s* John Garthside *b*   9 ,,
Tayler, Stephen, an infant *s* Lawrence Tayler, laborer *b*   18 ,,
Gressam, Hugh, labourer *b*   20 ,,
Parkins, John, glover *b*   24 ,,
Barnes, Mary, wife John Barnes, farmer *b*   24 ,,
Stubb, Elizabeth, wife Peter Stubb, glazier *b*   5 Aug.
Tayler, Mary, *d* Francis Tayler, glover *b*   14 ,,
Snoden, Rutland, Esqre. *b*   28 ,,
Howgrave, Elizabeth, infant *d* Alexander Howgrave, mercer *b*   28 ,,
Lawson, John, labourer *b*   8 Sept.
Smith, Dorothy, wife Hugh Smith *b*   16 Oct.
Hutchinson, Frances, widow *b*   21 ,,
Alesby, Priscilla, wife Robert Alesby *b*   2 Nov.
Attenell, Margaret, wife John Attenell *b*   26 Jan.
Beighton, Mary, *d* William Beighton, laborer *b*   20 Feb.
Wilkinson, William, an infant *b*   2 Mar.

[NOTE].—" See further for buryalls 1646 fol. 6 after this."

[Fol. 25*b*.]

MARRIAGES, 1654.

The consent of marriage between Edward Burr and Blanch Harnes both of Horncastle, both above the age of one and twenty yeares, was published these severall Lords dayes, that is to say upon the 7th day of July, the 14th day of July, and 21th day of July, 1654.

The said Edward Burr and Blanch Harnes were married at Langton the 8th of August, 1654.

[Signed] Ric: Ffilkin.

[The Contract of Matrimony betweene] Henry Foster of Horncastle, Joyner, and Elizabeth Phillipes of Langton by Horncastle, widdow, were published in the P'ish Church of Horncastle the severall Lords Dayes that is to say, the 30th of July, the 6th of Aug. and the 13th August, 1654.

[The Contract of Matrimony betweene] Adam Vinter of Horncastle, labourer, and Margery Key, of Tumby in the P'ish of Kickby-upon-Bayne were published three severall Lord's dayes in the P'ish of Horncastle, that is to say the 13th of August, the 20th of August, and the 27th of August.

The said Adam Vinter and Margery Key were married at Langton the 26th of September, 1654.

[Signed] Ric: Ffilkin.

[The Contract of Matrimony betweene] John West, shoemaker, and Jane Thompson, spinster, both of Horncastle were published these severall Lord's dayes in the P'ish Church of Horncastle aforesaid, that is to say the 17th of September, the 24th of September and the 1st of October, 1654.

The said John West and Jane Thompson were married at Langton the 26th of October, 1654.

The Contract of Matrimony betweene Peter Stubbs of Horncastle, and Elizabeth Melton of Panton [were published] the 3rd of September, the 10th and 17th of September [1654].

The Contract of Matrimony betweene George Elsten, taylor, and Ellen Stapleton, spinster, late of Horncastle were published the 10th, 17th and 24th of September [1654].

The Contract of Matrimony betweene William Vinter of Horncastle, labourer, and Mary Lawson of Edlington, spinster, were published the 15th, 22th and 29th of October [1654].

The Contract of Matrimony betweene William Taylor of Horncastle, tanner, and Ann Smith of Cumberworth, spinster, were published the 5th, the 12th, and the 19th of November [1654].

The Contract of Matrimony betweene Joseph Hamerton of Horncastle, glover, and Anthery Goose of the same, widdow, were published the 19th, and 26th of November, and the 8th of December [1654].

[Fol. 26a.

The Contract of Matrimony betweene Samuell Hamerton of Horncastle, tanner, and Frances Holbich, spinster, were published the 10th, the 17th and 24th of December and married at Boston by John Whiting, a Justice of the Peace, the second day of January 1654.

The Contract of Matrimony betweene John Dales of Horncastle, shoemoker, and Ellen Watt of Cunsby, spinster, were published the 31st of December, the 7th and 14th of January 1654.

The Contract of Matrimony betweene John Kendall of Boston, waterman, and Margery Tindall of Horncastle, spinster, were published the 7th, the 14th and 24th January, 1654.

1655.

The Contract of Matrimony betweene Thomas Thomlinson of Ashby puerorum, labourer, and Ellen Mitchell of Tumby, spinster, was published three severall Market dayes the 21th of April, 28th April and the 5th of May 1655.

The Contract of Matrimony betweene John Holdernes, labourer, and Frances Hutchinson, spinster, were published three severall Lord's dayes, the 24 of June, 10 of July ahd the 8 July, 1655.

The Contract of Matrimony betweene John Read and Margaret Nicolls were published the 24th of June, the first of July and the 8th of July 1655.

The said John Read and Margaret Nicholls were there married at Langton the 19th of July 1655.

Signed [Ric: ffilkin].

The Contract of Matrimony betweene Edward Bates of Gedney, and Dorcas Mayer of Horncastle were published the 24th of July, the 5th, and the 12th of August 1655.

The said Edward Bates and Dorcas Mayer were married at Louth the 28th day of August 1655.

The Contract of Matrimony betweene Thomas Thorpe, glover, and Elizabeth Stubs, spinster, late of Horncastle, were published three severall Lord's dayes the 18th and 25th of August and the second of September 1655.

The said Thomas Thorpe and Elizabeth Stubs were married at Little Sturton the 6th of September.

[Signed] ffra: Olinton.
al's ffines.

[NOTE]—"See further for Contracts and Marriages in the third leafe followinge."

[Fol. 26b.]
BIRTHS AND CHRISTENINGS, 1655.
Hollingworth, Judeth, d John Hollingworth, butcher, borne
23 March c   1 April

Page, Richard, *s* Thomas and Mary Page, currier, borne 5 March *c*	1 April
Daunse, Ann, *d* Stephen Daunse, glover, borne 23 March, 1654 *c*	1 ,,
Pacy, Richard, *s* Timothy and Elizabeth Pacy, carpenter, borne 28 March *c*	1 ,,
Enderby, John, *s* William and Susanna Enderby, borne 21 March 1654 *c*	8 ,,
Smith, William, *s* John and Alice Smith, ironmonger, borne 29 March *c*	26 ,,
White, Ann, *d* Thomas and Susanna White, weaver, borne 20 April *c*	29 ,,
Sherwin, Giles, *s* Robert and Ann Sherwin, yeoman, borne 20 November *c*	28 Dec. 1654.
Pell, Charles, *s* James and Marah Pell, ironmonger, borne 18 April *c*	2 May
Hamerton, William, *s* Thomas Hamerton, tauner, borne 15 April *c*	15 ,,
Beighton, Mary, *d* William and Ann Beighton, laborer, borne 6 June *c*	17 June
Simpson, Ann, *d* John and Ann Simpson, laborer, borne 9 July *c*	9 July
Tayler, Stephen, *s* Lawrence and Ann Tayler, laborer, borne 18 July *c*	16 ,,
Castledine, Alice, *d* William and Esther Castledine, chairmaker, borne 24 September *c*	30 Sept.
Alesby, Ann, *d* Robert and Priscilla Aylesby, taylour, borne 3 October *c*	7 Oct.
Plumpton, George, *s* George and ――――― Plumpton, basketmaker, borne 9 October *c*	21 ,,

[Fol. 27a.]

Vinter, Jane, *d* William and ―――― Vinter, labourer, borne 10 October *c*	21 ,,
Hamerton, Joseph, *s* Joseph and Anthery Hamerton, glover, borne 12 October *c*	30 ,,
Maddison, Ann, *d* William and Elizabeth Maddison, laborer, borne 18 October *c*	1 Nov.
Crastes, John, *s* Henry and Ann Crastes, cutler, borhe 5 November *c*	25 ,,
Tayler, John, *s* William and Ann Tayler, tanner, borne 11 November *c*	27 ,,
Elston, Elizabeth, *d* George and Ellen Elston, taylor, borne 6 November *c*	3 Dec.
Hamerton, John, *s* Robert and Ann Hamerton, glover, borne 9 December *c*	19 ,,
Tayler, Joseph, *s* Francis and Grace Tayler, glover, borne 15 December *c*	27 ,,
Howgrave, Ann, *d* Alexander and Mary Howgrave, mercer, borne 5 Decembrr *c*	26 ,,
Page, Daniell, *s* Richard and Susanna Page, currier, borne 1 Febrnary *c*	7 Feb.
Hutchinson, John, *s* John and Elizabeth Hutchinson, borne 17 January *c*	2 ,,
Richardson, Henry, *s* Moses and ――――― Richardson, labourer, borne 4 February *c*	10 ,,
Harriss, ――――― , *d* Hugh Harriss, laborer, borne 9 February *c*	24 ,,
Bradley, William, *s* Richard and Elizabeth Bradley, musition, borne 8 February *c*	17 ,,

[NOTE]—" Here ends Births and Christenings for 1655.

[Fol. 27b.]

BIRTHS AND CHRISTENINGS, 1656.

Hamerton, Samuell, s Samuell and Frances Hamerton, tanner, borne 23 April c	13 May
Garthside, John, s John and Christien Garthside, whitesmith, borne 29 April c	27 ,,
Peake, Thomas, s Edward and Margaret Peake, yeoman, borne borne 3 June c	16 June
Welsher, Richard, s John and Elizabeth Welsher, tanner, borne 13 June c	6 July
Tayler, Ann, d Lawrence Tayler, labourer, borne 27 July c	3 Aug.
Wilkinson, Herbert, s Herbert and Frances Wilkinson, labourer, borne 15 July c	10 ,,
Chester, Elizabeth, d William and Mary Chester, gardiner, borne 5 August c	8 ,,
Kettlewell, Appellina, d Thomas and ——— Kettlewell, scrivener, borne 6 August c	11 ,,
Wood, Richard, s Richard Wood, labourer, borne 15 August c	17 ,,
Francis, Hermon, s Hermon Francis, glover, borne 16 Aug. c	24 ,,
Smith, Benjamine, s John and Alice Smith, ironmonger, borne 10 August c	31 ,,
Fowler, Mary, d Robert and Mary Fowler, glover, borne 18 August c	24 ,,
Newman, Mary, d John and Penelope Newman, borne 20 August c	24 ,,
West, Jane, d John and ——— West, shoemaker, borne 23 August c	31 ,,
Mackris, Miles, s Thomas and Anne Mackris, shoemaker, borne 24 August c	31 ,,
Vrye, John, s Thomas and Katharine Vrye, mercer, borne 26 August c	30 ,,
Hill, Gabriell, s Gabriell and Anne Hill, tanner, borne 8 Sept. c	8 Oct.
Graves, Aspinall, s Ralph and Lidia Graves, sadler, borne 21 Sdptember c	2 ,,
Burton, Luke, s Luke and Mary Burton, woolen draper, borne 26 September c	7 ,,
Cater, Richard, s Richard and Mary Cater, chandler, borne 2 October c	16 ,,

[NOTE]—"See further 1656, folio 30 for births and Christenings."

[Fol. 28a.]

MARRIAGES.

The Contract of Matrimony betweene John Simpson, labourer, and Elizabeth Clapham, spinster, both of Horncastle, were published three several Lord's dayes the 19th of August, the 26th of August and the second of September 1655.

The said John Simpson and Elizabeth Clapham were married at Little Sturton the 13th of September, 1655.

[Signed] ffra. Clinton,
al's ffines.

The Contract of Matrimony betweene George Guising of Horncastle, mercer, and Elizabeth West of Reavsby, spinster, were published in Horncastle Church, three several Lord's dayes (that is to say) the 2 September, the 9th of September, and the 16th of September, 1655.

The said John Newman and Penelope [West] were married at Little Sturton the 4th of October 1655.

[Signed] ffra. Clinton,
al's ffines.

The Contract of Matrimony betweene Joshua Dawson of Horncastle, tanner, and Ann Stamblesby of Market Stainton, spinster, were published three severall Lord's dayes, in the Church of Horncastle, that is to say the 26th of August, the 2th of September and the 9th of September 1655.

The said Joshua **Dawson** and Ann Stamblesby were married at Little Sturton the 9th day of October 1655 by

[Signed] ffra. Clinton,
al's ffines.

The Contract of Matrimony betweene Jo'nathan **Bagnall** of Horncastle, shoemaker, and Jane **Porter**, spinster, both of Horncastle, were published three severall Lord's dayes, that is to say the 2th of September, the 9th of September, and the 16th of September, 1655.

The said Jo'nathan **Bagnall** and Jane **Porter** were married at Little Sturton the 10th of October 1655 by

ffra. Clinton,
al's ffines.

[Fol. 28b.]

The Contract of Matrimony betweene Thomas **Mackris** of Horncastle, and Ann **Burch** of Edlington were published three severall Lord's dayes in the P'ish Church of Horncastle, that is to say the 28 day of October, the 4th of November and the 11th of November 1655.

The said Thomas **Mackris** and Ann **Burch** were married at Little Sturton the 15th day of November by

[Sigeed] ffra Clinton,
al's ffines.

The Contract of Matrimony betweene Peter **Stubbs** and Ellen **Burch**, both of Horncastle, have been published in Horncastle Church three severall Lord's dayes, that is to say the 4th, the 11th and the 18th of November 1655.

The said Peter **Stubbs** and Ellen **Burch** were married at Little Sturton the 27th of November 1655 by

[Signed] ffra. Clinton,
al's ffines.

The Contract of Matrimony betweene John **Vrye**, gent., and Alice **West**, widow, both of Horncastle, were published three severall Lord's dayes in the Church of Horncastle the ———, ———, ———.

The said John **Vrye** and Alice **West** were married at Little Sturton the 27th day of November 1655 by

[No Signature]

MARRIAGES 1656 AND SOME 1655.

The Contract of Matrimony betweene William **Evers** of Horncastle and Sarah **Greene** of Thornton were published in the Church of Horncastle three severall Lord's dayes, that is to say the 3 of February, the 10th of February and the 17th of February 1655.

The said William **Evers** and Sarah **Greene** were married at Little Sturton the 27th of March 1656 by

[No Signature]

The Contract of Matrimony betweene Arthur **Vinter** and Elizabeth **Hanson** were published the 3th, 10th, and 17th February 1655, in the Church of Horncastle.

The said Arthur **Vinter** and Elizabeth **Hanson** were married at ——— the 19th February 1655.

[Fol. 29a.]

The Contract of Matrimony between Robert **Alsby** and Deborah **Woods** was published in Horncastle Church the 27 of January and the 3 and 10 of February 1656.

The said Robert **Alsby** and Deborah **Woods** were married at Little Sturton the 22 of Feb. 1656.

The Contract of Matrimony betweene Robert **Gibson** and Rosamond **Marver** was published in Horncastle Church the 12 : 19 : and 26th of Octob., 1656.

> The said Robert **Gibson** and Rosamond **Mawer** were married at Little Sturton the 12th of November 1656 By mee
>
>   [Signed] ffra : Clinton,
>   al's ffines.

The Contract of Matrimony betweene Henry **Barker** of Halton Holegate, butcher, and Alice **Francis** of Horncastle, spinster, were published the 14, 21 and 28th of September 1656.

The Contract of Matrimony betweene John **Gentle**, labourer, and Cicily **Stamp**, spinster, late of Horncastle were published the 19th and 26th of October and 2 of November 1656.

The Contract of Matrimony betweene Hugh **Maultby** of Boston, painter, and Ann **Knubley** of this P'ish, spinster, were published the 22th, and 22th of June and 6th July 1656.

The Contract of Matrimony betweene John **Hughenson** and Elizabeth **Coulham**, spinster, both of Maring-on-the-hill as members of this P'ish, were published the 29th June, the 6th and 13th of July 1656.

[Fol. 29b.]
1656.

The Contract of Matrimony betweene William **Westeby** and Sarah **Nicholson** were published three several Lord's dayes in the P'ish Church of Horncastle, that is to say the 13th of April, 20 and 27th of April.

> The said William **Westeby** and Sarah **Nicholson** were married at Birkwood in the P'ish of Reavesby the 15th day of May 1656. By me
>
>   [Signed] Nehemiah Rawson.

William **Sands** and Joane **Porter** the Contract of Matrimony betweene them was published in Horncastle Church the 13, 20 and 27th day of ———— 1656.

> The said William **Sands** and Joane **Porter** were married at Little Sturton the 9th May, 1656.

The Contract of Matrimony betweene Edward **Grayson** and Margaret **Lawrence**, widow, was published in Horncastle Church the 20, 27th of April and 4th of May 1656.

> The said Edward **Grayson** and Margaret **Lawrence** were married at Little Sturton the ———— of May 1656.

The Contract of Matrimony betweene Robert **Tayler** of Horncastle, glover, and Jane **Pacy** of Wester Keal, spinster, was published in Horncastle Church the 13, 20 and 27th of April 1656.

> The said Robert **Tayler** and Jane **Pacy** were married at Raithby the 3th of June 1656.

The Contract of Matrimony betweene John **Attewell** of Horncastle, glover, and Alice **Davy** of West Ashby was published in Horncastle Church the 18th and 25th of May and the first of June 1656.

> The said John **Attenell** and Alice **Davy** were married at Horncastle the 3th of June 1656 By
>
>   [Signed] Nehemiah Rawson.

The Contract of Matrimony betweene Hugh **Smith** [and] Margery **Whitliffe** was published in Horncastle Church the 11th, 18th and 25th of May 1656.

> The said Hugh **Smith** and Margery **Whitliffe** were married at Horncastle the first of July 1656. By me
>
>   [Signed] ffra. Clinton,
>   al's ffines.

[Fol. 30a.]

The Contract of Matrimony betweene Thomas Woodthorpe, tanner, and Ann Martindale, spinster, both of Horncastle have been published three several Lord's dayes (that is to say) the 25 October the 2 and 9th of November 1656.

The said Thomas Woodthorp and Ann Martindale were married the 25th day of November 1656 at Malbush Enderby By mee [Signed] Jos. Whiting.

The Contract of Matrimony betweene Joseph Rapham of this P'ish, butcher, and Elizabeth Atkinson of Halton Holegate, spinster, the 14th 21th, and 28th of December 1656.

The Contract of Matrimony betweene William Vinter, labourer, and Jane Gresham, widow, both of this P'ish were published January 25th, the 1th and 8th of February 1656.

The Contract of Matrimony betweene John Kelsey of Ashby, Horncastle, labourer, and Deborah Brinkhill of Belshford, spinster, were published the several Market dayes in Horncastle Market, the 14th, 21th and 28th of February 1656.

The Contract of Matrimony betweene Jeremiah Browne and Isabel Pibus both of Horncastle were published the 8, 15, 22th of March 1656.

John West and Mary Peares both of the P'ish were published the 8, 15, 22th of March 1656.

" Note that where you finde the Contracts of Marriages Regestred and not the Marriages themselves, such p'sons were not Marryed in Horncastle."

[Fol. 30b.]

BIRTHS AND CHRISTENINGS, 1656.

Holdernes, Alice, d John and Frances Holdernes, laborer, borne 18 October c	26 Oct.
Osborne, William, s John and Alice Osborne, laborer, borne 28th October c	28 "
Pell, Ann, d James and Marah Pell, ironmonger, borne 11th November c	12 Nov.
Thorpe, Elizabeth, d Thomas and Elizabeth Thorpe, glover, borne 13th November c	26 "
Page, John, s Thomas and Margaret Page, currier, borne 10th December c	11 Dec.
Danks, Susanna, d Philip and Elizabeth Danks, bricklayer, borne 2 December c	1 Jan.
Shotten, Mary, d Edward Shotten, shoemaker, borne 30 December c	19 Jan.
Vinter, John, s Arthur and Elizabeth Vinter, tanner, borne 8 January c	1 Feb.
Parrish, John, s John and Ellen Parrish, taylor, borne 15 January c	5 "
Kerke, John, s William and Mary Kerke, the younger, tinker, borne 24 January c	8 "
Danse, Ellen, d Stephen and Mary Danse, glover, borne 14 January c	6 "
Westeby, John, s William and Sarah Westeby, painter, borne 4 February c	10 "
Chapman, John, s John and Mary Chapman, ironmonger, borne 13 February [date of c wanting].	
Simpson, Alice, d William and Alice Simpson, tanner, borne the of February, c	1 Mar.
Maultby, George, s William Maultby, laborer, borne 10 March c	15 Mar.
Maddison, William, s William and Elizabeth Maddison, laborer, borne 3 March c	15 "

Stubbs, Mary, *d* Peter and Elizabeth Stubbs, the younger, borne 17 March *c* ... 20 Mar.

Tayler, William, *s* William and Ann Tayler, the younger, borne the — of March *c* ... 22 ,,

[NOTE]—Here endeth Births and Christenings, 1656.

[Fol. 31*a*.]

BURIALLS, 1656.

Peake, Mary, widdow *b* ... 27 ,,
Wilkinson, William, an infant *b* ... 13 April
Francis, Frances, widdow *b* ... 4 June
Ellis, Mark, *s* of one Rich : Ellis of Scothorn, a Chapman *b* ... 13 ,,
Fowler, Ann, an infant *b* ... 16 ,,
Stubban, William, an infant *b* ... 17 ,,
Tayler, Grace, *d* Francis Tayler *b* ... 28 ,,
Hamerton, John, the lesse, a tanner *b* ... 1 July
Tayler, John, *s* Francis Tayler *b* ... 4 ,,
Bennett, John, a yong man *b* ... 11 ,,
Hawley, William, laborer *b* ... 16 ,,
Lawson, Ellen, widdow *b* ... 23 ,,
Tayler, George, *s* Francis Tayler *b* ... 4 Aug.
Newby, Judeth, a spinster *b* ... 22 ,,
Hollingworth, Judeth, an infant *b* ... 24 ,,
Woodthorp, Margaret, wife Thomas Woodthorp *b* ... 27 ,,
Frankis, Elizabeth, an infant *b* ... 30 ,,
Frankis, John, an infant *b* ... 31 ,,
Sympson, Alice, an infant *b* ... 11 Sept.
Plumpton, George, an infant *b* ... 13 ,,
Pell, John, *s* James Pell *b* ... 4 Oct.
West, Jane, an infant *b* ... 5 ,,
Pinchbeck, Nehemiah, a yong man *b* ... 15 ,,
Freston, Ann, an infant *b* ... 16 ,,
Hamerton, Samuel, an infant *b* ... 18 ,,
Plumpton, Job, an infant *b* ... 18 ,,
Pasmore, Mary, wife William Pasmore *b* ... 21 ,,
Bennett, Robert, a yong youth *b* ... 22 ,,
Johnson, Mary, an infant *b* ... 23 ,,
Ridg, Mary, widdow *b* ... 25 ,,
Vinter, Jane, an infant *b* ... 26 ,,
Crastes, John, an infant *b* ... 26 ,,
Burwell, Elizabeth, widdow *b* ... 28 ,,
Osborn, William, an infant *b* ... 28 ,,
Osborn, Alice, wife John Osborn *b* ... 29 ,,
Snelland, Christopher, laborer *b* ... 6 Nov.
Gibson, Marmaduke, a youth *b* ... 8 ,,
Hodgson, Robert, a youth *b* ... 8 ,,
Holderness, Alice, an infant *b* ... 9 ,,
Howgrave, Ann, an infant *b* ... 10 ,,
Hancock, Stephen, a barbour *b* ... 14 ,,
Milner, Daniell, a youth *b* ... 18 ,,
Bradley, William, an infant *b* ... 18 ,,
Milner, Elizabeth, a yong girle *b* ... 20 ,,
White, John, a yong youth *b* ... 21 ,,
Bitchfield, Sarah, an infant *b* ... 21 ,,
Vrye, John, an infant *b* ... 25 ,,
Pell, Ann, an infant *b* ... 28 ,,
Coupland, Katharine, wife George Coupland, baker *b* ... 1 Dec.

[Fol. 31*b*.]

Beane, Rosamond, late wife Thomas Beane, deceased *b* ... 1 ,,

Howgrave, Mary, wife Alexander Howgrave, mercer *b*	7	Dec.
Dales, Mary, an infant *b*	8	,,
Thorp, Elizabeth, an infant *b*	14	,,
Page, John, an infant *b*	14	,,
———, Joane, a maid servant *b*	30	,,
Danks, Elizabeth, a yong virgin *b*	31	,,
Hamerton, Frances, wife Samuel Hamerton, tanner *b*	2	Jan.
Kettlewell, Rebecca, a yong virgin *b*	2	,,
Kettlewell, Appellina, an infant *b*	6	,,
West, Jane, wife John West, shoemaker *b*	7	,,
Smith, John, taylor *b*	18	,,
Pacy, Richard, an infant *b*	28	,,
Robinson, Thomas, weaver *b*	9	Feb.
Howell, Katherine, widdow *b*	12	,,
Milner, Robert, kilne keeper *b*	14	,,
Tayler, Ann, wife William Tayler, the elder, tanner *b*	25	,,
Danks, Susanna, an infant *b*	25	,,
Kerk, John, an infant *b*	2	Mar.
Burton, Luke, an infant *b*	3	,,
Stubbs, Mary, an infant *b*	8	,,
Simpson, Elizabeth, wife John Simpson, laborer *b*	8	,,
Stamp, Peter, glover *b*	14	,,
West, Thomas, blacksmith *b*	14	,,

CONTRACTS AND MARRIAGES, 1657.

The Contract of Matrimony betweene John Osborn of this P'ish and Mary Lathrop of Nether Toynton was published the 12, 19, 26th of April, 1657.

These p'sons were married at [place wanting].

The Contract of Matrimony betweene John Chamberlane and Mary Hancock both of this P'ish was published the 19, 26 April, and 3 May 1657.

These p'sons were married at [place wanting].

The Contract of Matrimony betweene William Lands of this P'ish and Mary Halliday of Screlsby was published 26 April, 3 and 10th of May 1657.

These p'sons were married at Langton next Horncastle, 4th July 1657.

[Fol. 32a.]

The Contract of Matrimony betweene Thomas Chapman of West Ashby and Elizabeth Waller of this P'ish, was published 26 April, 3 and 10th of May 1657.

These p'sons were married at Langton by Horncastle.

The Contract of Matrimony betweene Alexander Howgrave, mercer, of this P'ish and Elizabeth Allenson of St. Lawrence Lane, London was published the 3, 10, and 17th of May 1657.

These P'sons were married at London.

The Contract of Matrimony betweene Henry Almond and Elizabeth Thorold both of this P'ish was published the 14, 21 and 28th of June 1657.

These p'sons were married at Langton by Horncastle the 2th of July 1657.

The Contract of Matrimony betweene William Stanton of this P'ish and Priscilla Kilborne of Louth was published the 21, 28 June and 5th of July 1657.

Noe Certificate.

The Contract of Matrimony betweene Richard Browne and Anne Francis both of this P'ish was published the 28 June and 5th and 12th of July 1657.

    These p'sons were married at [place wanting].

Ralph Clapham and Ellen Nicholls both of this P'ish was published the 12, 19 and 26th of July 1657.

    These p'sons were married at Horncastle the 20th October 1657.

Edward Chambers of Swinshead and Mary Gunby of this P'ish was published the 16, 23 and 30th of August 1657.

    These p'sons were married at Langton next Horncastle the 6th of Sept. 1657.

William Lyell and Katherine Snelland was published the 23, 30th of August and 6th of Sept. 1657.

    These p'sons were married at Langton next Horncastle the 8th of September 1657.

Samuell Hamerton of this P'ish and Susanna Woodthorp of Maring-on-the-hill was published the 6, 13 and 20th of Sept. 1657.

    These P'sons were married at Reavesby ffirst by Nehemiah Rawson Esqre., Justice of Peace, and after married by Mr. Williams Minister of Reavesby the 6 of October 1657.

James Preston of this P'ish, and Alice Wasse of Bullingbrooke was published the 13, 20 and 27 of Sept. 1657,

    (Noe Certificate).

George Mitten of Minting and Susanna Newman of this P'ish was published the 27 of Sept. and 4 and 11th of October 1657.

    These p'sons were married at Minting the 22th Oct. 1657.

John Tayler of Consby and ffaith Thorp of this P'ish was published the 18, 25 Oct. and first November 1657.

    These p'sons were married at Horncastle the 12th of November.

       [Fol. 32b.]

George Byron of Lincoln and Margaret Wright of this P'ish was published the 25th of October the first and 8th of November 1657.

    These p'sons were married the 24th of November 1657 at Horncastle.

John Wade of Marton by Horncastle and Elizabeth Tipping of this P'ish was published the 25th October, the first and 8th of November 1657.

    These p'sons were married at Marton aforesd. the 3th of November 1657.

Richard Bonner and Joane Parker both of this P'ish was published the 25th of October, the first and 8th of November 1657.

    These p'sons were married at Horncastle the 10th of Dec. 1657.

John Parker of Moorby and Margaret ffookes of Hagworthingham was published in the Market place of Horncastle the 19th, 26th of Sept. and the 3th of October 1657.

    These p'sons were married at Mavis Enderby the 28th of December 1657.

William Watson of Bardney and Mary Markby of this P'ish was published the 15, 22 and 29th of November 1657.

    These p'sons were married at Thimbleby the 15th of December 1657. (Noe Certificate).

Thomas Hamerton and Isabell Hamerton both of this P'ish was published the 6, 13, and 20th of December 1657.

    These p'sons were married at Horncastle the 7th day of January 1657.

William **Nightscales** of this P'ish and Mary Dixon of Ashby next Horncastle was published the 13, 20, and 27th of December 1657.

These p'sons were married at Thornton the 10th of January 1657.

William **Watson** of this P'ish and Jane Beeston of Nether Toynton were published the 10, 17 and 24th of January 1657.

These p'sons were married at Horncastle the 28th January 1657.

John **Johnson** and Martha **Siser** both of this P'ish was published the 31th of Jan., and 7 and 14th of Feb. 1657.

These P'sons were married at Horncastle the 28th of Feb. 1657.

[Fol. 38a.]

John **Dawson** of this P'ish and Susanna Shaw of Stickford was published the 31th of January, the 7th and 14th of January 1657.

These p'sons were married at Horncastle the 28th of Feb. 1657.

Jo: Smith and Abigail Hussey were published in Horncastle Market the 13, 20 and 27 February.

These p'sons were married at Horncastle by Mr. Obadiah How the 15th of March 1657.

BIRTHS AND CHRISTENINGS, 1657.

Bagnall, John, *s* Jonathan and Jane Bagnall, shoemaker, borne 10th April *c*	12 April
Pacy, Elisabeth, *d* Tymothie and Elizabeth Pacy, carpenter, borne 3th May *c*	10 May
Carr, Walter, *s* Thomas and May Carr, shoemaker, borne 19th May *c*	23 ,,
Freston, Mary, *d* Richard and Deborah Freston, butcher, borne 25th May *c*	81 ,,
Greene, William, *s* Robt. and Sarah Greene, labourer, borne 5th June *c*	7 June
Graysen, Mary, *d* Edward and Margaret Graysen, yeoman, borne 21th May *c*	21 ,,
Fetherstone, Ann, *d* William and Ann Fetherstone, *al's* Franks, shoemaker, borne 17th June *c*	23 ,,
Alesby, Jane, *d* Robert and Debora Alesby, taylor, borne 1th July *c*	13 July
Craste, Phebee, *d* Henry and Ann Craste, cutler, borne 25th July *c*	9 Aug.
Woodthorp, Thomas, *s* Thomas and Ann Woodthorp, borne 9th September *c*	13 Sept.
Gentle, Ann, *d* John and Cicily Gentle, laborer, borne 10th September *c*	13 ,,
Guising, Mary, *d* George and Elizabeth Guising, mercer, borne 6th September *c*	17 ,,
Plumpton, Nicholas, *s* George Plumpton, basket maker, borne 26 August *c*	27 ,,

[Fol. 38b.]

Etherington, Priscilla, *d* John and Joane Etherington, tanner borne 26th August *c*	27 ,,
Holdernes, Frances, *d* John and Frances Holdernes, gardiner, borne 26 September *c*	11 Oct.
Smith, Jeremiah, *s* John and Alice Smith, ironmonger, borne 6th October *c*	11 ,,
Watson, William, *s* William and Mary Watson, laborer, borne 24th September *c*	11 ,,
Tayler, Sarah, *d* Francis Tayler, glover, borne 29th Sept. *c*	15 ,,
Sands, Alice, *d* William and Joane Sands, laborer, borne 10th October *c*	25 ,,

Gibson, John, *s* Robert and Frances Gibson, butcher, borne 13th November *c*   22 Nov.

Dales, Ann, *d* John and Ellen Dales, translater, borne 6th November *c*   22 ,,

Maidens, Elizabeth, *d* Edmund and Margaret Maidens, taylor, borne 14th November *c*   22 ,,

Ivers, Richard, *s* William and Sarah Ivers, shoemaker, borne 15th November *c*   7 Dec.

Burton, Thomas, *s* Luke and Mary Burton, woollen draper, borne 8th December *c*   13 ,,

Goode, Samuell, *s* John and Margery Goode, tayler, borne 4th December *c*   13 ,,

Hill, Bridget, *d* Gabriell and Ann Hill, borne 25 December *c*   27 ,,

Gentle, Thomas, *s* Benjamine and Elizabeth Gentle, laborer, borne 12th December *c*   20 ,,

Bonner, Elizabeth, *d* William and Elizabeth Bonner, laborer, borne 24 December *c*   10 Jan.

Dawson, Mary, *d* Thomas and Magdalen Dawson, laborer, borne 13 January *c*   24 ,,

Parker, John, *s* Thomas and Alice Parker, glover, borne 10th January *c*   24 ,,

[Fol. 34a.]

Peares, Steven, *s* Ensoby and Ann Peares, currier, borne 24th January *c*   31 ,,

Batty, Elizabeth, *d* Francis and Elizabeth Batty, barber, borne 19 January *c*   31 ,,

Kerke, Ralph, *s* William and Mary Kerke, the younger, tinker, borne 2 February *c*   7 Feb.

Thorp, Thomas, *s* Thomas and Elizabeth Thorp, glover, borne 20th February *c*   28 ,,

Page, Nicholas, *s* Richard and Susanna Page, currier, borne 2th March *c*   5 Mar.

Enderby, Susanna, *d* William and Susanna Enderby, laborer, borne 28th February *c*   7 ,,

Howgrave, George, *s* Alexander and Elizabeth Howgrave, mercer, borne 15 March *c*   15 ,,

Browne, Elizabeth, *d* Jeremiah and Isabel Browne, whitesmith, borne 6th March *c*   21 ,,

Burwell, Elizabeth, *d* James Burwell, shoemaker, borne 9th March *c*   21 ,,

Osborne, Roger, *s* John and Mary Osborne, laborer, borne 16th March *c*   16 ,,

BURIALLS, 1657.

Huddleston, Frances, an infant *b*   10 April

Baxter, Edward, shoemaker *b*   14 ,,

Graves, Lawrence, baliste *b*   26 ,,

Westeby, Edward, painter *b*   16 May

Birch, John, a young man *b*   6 June

Harriss, Alice, an infant *b*   8 ,,

Pinder, Elizabeth, a yong girle *b*   9 ,,

Newman, Mary *b*   23 July

Lyell, Susanna, wife William Lyell, tinker *b*   10 Aug.

Wade, William, yeoman *b*   27 ,,

Birch, Ellen, spinster *b*   31 ,,

Hamerton, John, an infant *b*   2 Sept.

Smith, William, mason *b*   13 ,,

Browne, Thomas, beel maker *b*   15 ,,

Clark, Anne, an infant *b*   6 Oct.

Cooke, Hamond, musition *b*   20 ,,

Cheesbroo, Richard, tayler *b*	28 Oct.
Mackris, Barbara, wife Edward Mackris, tanner *b*	29 ,,
Johnson, Elizabeth, wife Martin Johnson, tanner *b*	8 Nov.
[Fol. 84*b*.]	
Smith, Hugh, tanner *b*	5 ,,
Watson, William, an infant *b*	12 ,,
Watson, Mary, wife William Watson, labourer *b*	19 ,,
Peares, Sarah, wife William Peares, shoemaker *b*	6 Dec.
Slater, Ellen, widdow *b*	7 ,,
Castledine, William, chairmaker *b*	21 ,,
Gibson, John, an infant *b*	22 ,,
Guising, Alice, wife William Guising, mercer *b*	27 ,,
Parker, Dorothy, wife Samuell Parker, weaver *b*	27 ,,
Hodgson, Thomas, and a yong man *b*	29 ,,
Shotten, Charles, shoemaker *b*	10 Jan.
Burton, Mary, wife Matthew Burton, carpenter *b*	10 ,,
Enderby, James, taylor *b*	13 ,,
Clarke, Robert, taylor *b*	16 ,,
Freston, Mary, an infant *b*	23 ,,
Peares, Richard, carpenter *b*	26 ,,
Parker, John, an infant *b*	7 Feb.
Thompson, Ellen, wife Robert Thompson, laborer *b*	8 ,,
Stevenson, Thomas, butcher *b*	22 ,,
Page, Nicholas, an infant *b*	10 Mar.
Lowe, George, musition *b*	11 ,,
Parrish, John, an infant *b*	14 ,,
Howgrave, John, an infant *b*	16 ,,
Osborne, Roger, an infant *b*	17 ,,
Embling, Elisabeth, spinster *b*	24 ,,
Births and Christenings, 1658.	
Almond, Ann, *d* Henry and Elisabeth Almond, taylor, borne 26th March *c*	27 ,,
Stubbs, Peter, *s* Peter and Elisabeth Stubbs, the yonger, glasier, borne 30th March *c*	7 April
Newman, Ann, *d* John and Penelope Newman, laborer, 12th March *c*	11 ,,
Laines, Margaret, *d* William and Mary Laines, taylor, borne 12th April *c*	18 ,,
Danks, John, *s* Phillip and Elizabeth Danks, bricklayer, borne 21 April *c*	2 May
[Fol. 85*a*.]	
Hindes, Frances, *d* Thomas and Frances Hindes, laborer, borne 18th April *c*	22 April
Fowler, Jane, *d* Robert and Mary Fowler, glover, borne 25 June *c*	27 June
Johnson, Elizabeth, *d* Roger and Grace Johnson, laborer, borne 30 July *c*	2 Aug.
Dymook, Frances, *d* of Mr. Edward Dymook the yonger, of Screlsby and Abigail his wife, borne 20 August *c*	24 ,,
Cater, Robert, *s* Richard and Mary Cater, ironmonger, borne 20th August *c*	18 Sept.
Witten, George, *s* George and Susanna Witten, weaver, borne 7th September *c*	9 ,,
Westeby, Rebecca, *d* William and Sarah Westeby, painter, borne 7th September *c*	14 ,,
Mackris, Thomas, *s* Thomas and Ann Mackris, cordwiner, borne 22th September *c*	3 Oct.
Simpson, Richard, *s* William and Alice Simpson, tanner, borne 4th October *c*	10 ,,

—Gibson, Mary, *d* Robert Gibson, deceased, and Rosamond his
    wife, borne 5th October *c*   10 Oct.

—Pell, James, *s* James and Marah Pell, ironmonger, borne 5th
    October *c*   6 ,,

—Nightscales, Richard, *s* William and Mary Nightscales,
    tanner, borne 18 November *c*   25 Nov.

— Burton, William, *s* Luke and Mary Burton, woolen draper,
    borne 2th January *c*   6 Jan.

- Parrish, Mary, *d* John and Hellen Parrish, taylor, borne 7th
    December *c*   6 ,,

- Tayler, Mary, *d* Lawrence and Ann Tayler, laborer, borne 5th
    Janvary *c*   9 ,,

—Clapham, Hellen, *d* Ralph and Hellen Clapham, laborer,
    borne 5th January *c*   9 ,,

- Dawson, Mary, *d* Joshua and Ann Dawson, tanner, borne 11
    November, but not known to be baptized.

- Smith, Rebecca, *d* John and Alice Smith, ironmonger, borne
    14 February *c*   21 Feb.

- Vinter, Mary, } *dd* William Vinter, laborer, borne 23th Feb. *c*   23 ,,
- Vinter, Jane, }

—Smith, Thomas, *s* Thomas and Elizabeth Smith, bricklayer,
    borne 25th February *c*   6 Mar.

                  [Fol. 85b.]

—Johnson, John, *s* John and Martha Johnson, a glasse seller,
    borne 1th March *c*   6 ,,

—Tayler, Urscilla, *d* William and Ann Tayler, borne 4th Mar. *c*   10 ,,

- Howgrave, Thomas, *s* Alexander and Elizabeth Howgrave,
    mercer, borne 7th March *c*   6 ,,

         Here endeth Births and Christenings, 1658.

     CONTRACTS AND MARRIAGES, 1658.

    William Tayler of Horncastle, and Mary Johnson of Thorp-in-the-
Marsh, were published the 28th of March, 4 and 11th of April, 1658.

    Edward Hodgson of Tattershall and Mary Birch of Horncastle were
published the 28th of March, the 4th and 11th of April 1658.
          These p'sons were married at Thimbleby the 11th of May by
          Mr. Martin Bennett.

    Robert Butler of Ashby by Horncastle and Jane Hickson of
Horncastle were published the 18th of April 25th April and 2th of May
1658.
          These p'sons were married at Thimbleby by the above sd.
          Martin Bennett, the 18th of May 1658.

    Nathaniell Foster of Langton by Horncastle and Ann Looking of
Horncastle were published the 20, 27th of June and 4th July 1658.
          These p'sons were married the 28th July 1658.

    John Harding and Bridget Stevenson were married the 7th
December 1658.

    Hastens Markby and Ann Wright were married 8th of February 1658.

    Danyell Haward and Mary Enderby were married 14th of February,
1658.

    William Shepley, gent., and Ann Garthside, widdow, were maryed
the 25th of January by John Hodgson, Rector of Donnington-upon-bane,
as appeares by a Certificate under the hand of the said John Hodgson in
the pr'sence of John Skipwith of Louth
          ffrances Garthside
          Mary Wilson and
          Amy Ward.

[Fol. 36a.]

BURIALLS, 1658.

Almond, Ann, an infant *b*	28	Mar.
Wilkinson, Herbert, labourer *b*	31	,,
Garthside, Francis, tanner and inholder *b*	4	April
Johnson, Alice, servant to John Simpson *b*	6	,,
Woodthorpe, Elizabeth, an infant *b*	9	,,
Stubbs, Peter, an infant *b*	11	,,
Gibson, Robert, the younger, butcher *b*	18	,,
Tayler, Jane, wife of Robert Tayler, glover *b*	20	,,
Burwell, James, shoemaker *b*	25	,,
Gillam, Thomas, a little boy *b*	1	May
Holdernes, Joane, widdow *b*	4	,,
Burwell, ——, an infant *b*	6	,,
Wells, Julian, widow *b*	8	,,
Page, Amy, widow *b*	18	,,
Wilkinson, William, a little boy *b*	18	,,
Enderby, Susanna, an infant *b*	22	,,
Markby, Richard, butcher *b*	30	,,
Burton, Matthew, carpenter *b*	3	June
Palmer, Peter an Exciseman *b*	33	,,
Pibus, Thomas, a yong man *b*	8	July
Palmer, William, son of the aforesd. Peter Palmer *b*	9	,,
Baren, Alice, widow *b*	18	,,
Wright, Ann, wife of Gabriel Wright, glover *b*	1	Aug.
Baldam, ——, widow *b*	18	,,
Snoden, Mrs. Frances, widdow *b*	29	,,
Kerk, William, tinker *b*	8	Sept.
Burton, Robert, taylor *b*	18	,,
Witten, George, an infant *b*	22	,,
Bitchfield, John, laborer *b*	3	Oct.
Ashton, John, shoemaker *c*	5	,,
Harding, Frances, wife of John Harding, p'ish clerke *b*	17	,,
Westeby, Rebecca, an infant *b*	29	,,
Tayler, William, the elder, tanner *b*	7	Nov.
Kerk, Clement, translater *b*	7	,,
Daunce, Mary, wife of Stephen Daunce, glover *b*	10	,,
Massey, Mary, wife of John Massey of Woodall, yeoman *b*	15	,,
Alesby, Robert, taylor *b*	27	,,
Hines, Frances, an infant *b*	28	,,
Feltrick, Mary, spinster, servant to James Pell *b*	29	,,
Burwell, William, an infant *b*	5	Dec.
Tayler, Richard, glover *b*	6	,,
Hill, Gabriell, tanner *b*	6	,,
Nightscales, Richard, an infant *b*	8	,,
Dawson, John, a youth about 8 yeares of age deceased in the house of John Goode a taylor *b*	10	,,
Gibson, Mary, an infant *b*	19	,,
Lowe, George, a yong youth *b*	20	,,
Harris, ——, wife of Hugh Harris, labourer *b*	23	,,
Harris, Lettis, an infant *b*	30	,,
Salmon, George, labourer *b*	5	Jan.

[Fol. 36b.]

Bagnall, John, infant *b*	6	,,
Fowler, Hellen, widow *b*	7	,,
Harriss, Hellen, wife John Harriss, laborer *b*	27	,,
Burton, Mary, wife Luke Burton, woelen draper *b*	4	Feb.
Nicholson, John, *s* John Nicholson, laborer *b*	15	,,
Peake, Edward, Towne Baliffe *b*	17	,,

— Parker, Samuel, weaver *b*   18 Feb.
— Roades, Elizabeth, widow *b*   21 ,,
— Browne, Elizabeth, an infant *b*   22 ,,
— Vinter, Jane, an infant *b*   25 ,,
— Gresham, Edward, a little youth *b*   26 ,,
— Mackris, Thomas, an infant *b*   26 ,,
— Waddingham, Thomas, an apprentice to John Goode, taylor *b*   1 Mar.
— Wright, Ann, wife of Thomas Wright, laborer *b*   2 ,,
— Burton, Thomas, an infant *b*   5 ,,
— Hanson, John, carpenter *b*   11 ,,
— Tayler, Ursoilla, an infant *b*   11 ,,
— Attinell, Christopher, shoemaker *b*   18 ,,

Here endeth buryalls 1658.

BIRTHES AND CHRISTENINGS, 1659.

— Hill, Bridget, *d* Gabriel and Ann Hill, tanner, deceased, borne 6 April *c*   10 April
— Parker, Elizabeth, *d* Thomas and Alice Parker, glover, borne 1 April *c*   10 ,,
— Hamerton, Susanna, *d* Samuel and Susanna Hamerton, tanner, borne 12 April *c*   17 ,,
— Vinter, William, *s* Arthur and Elizabeth Vinter, tanner, borne 17 April *c*   24 ,,
— Hamerton, Mary, *d* Robert and Ann Hamerton, glover, borne 24 April *c*   24 ,,
— Guising, George, *s* George and Elizabeth Guising, borne 16 June *c*   19 ,,
— Smith, Margaret, *d* William Smith, bricklayer, borne 24 July *c*   31 ,,
— Almond, Thomas, *s* Henry and Elizabeth Almond, taylor, borne 4 Aug. *c*   7 Aug.
— Shotten, Susanna, *d* Edward and Susanna Shotten, shoemaker, borne 15 Aug. *c*   21 ,,
— Fisher, William, *s* Christopher and Elizabeth Fisher, whitesmith, borne 2 Aug. *c*   28 ,,
— Thorp, Mary, *d* Thomas and Elizabeth Thorpe, glover, borne 16 September *c*   25 ,,

[Fol. 37a.]

— Bonner, Sasanna, *d* Richard Bonner, laborer, borne 10 Oct. *c*   17 ,,
— Hollingworth, Richard, *s* Richard and Susanna Hollingworth, laborer, borne 7 Oct. *c*   30 ,,
— Graves, Samuel, *s* Ralph, and Lidia Graves, sadler, borne 31 October *c*   1 Nov.
— Stubbs, Thomas, *s* Peter and Elizabeth Stubbs the younger, glazier, borne 1st April *c*   6 ,,
— Enderby, Robert, *s* William and Susanna Enderby, laborer, borne 17 October *c*   13 ,,
— Chester, Anna, *d* William and Mary Chester, gardiner, borne 29 November *c*   8 Dec.
— Bocock, Mary, *d* John and Mary Bocock, borne 7th Dec. *c*   7 ,,
— Lanes, Mary, *d* William and Mary Lanes, taylor, borne 11 December *c*   13 ,,
— Bradley, Robert, *s* Richard and Elizabeth Bradley, musition, borne 15 December *c*   13 ,,
— Markby, Hellen, *d* Haslene and Margaret Markby, butcher, borne 14th December *c*   18 ,,
— Carr, Olive, *d* Thomas and Mary Carr, shoemaker, borne 10th December *c*   25 ,,
— Vinter, Mary, *d* William Vinter, laborer *c*   28 Feb.
— Parker, Rebecca, *d* Edward and Ann Parker, taylor, borne 6th January *c*   8 Jan.

Gentle, Sarah, *d* John and Emily Gentle, laborer, borne 5th January *c*	8 Jan.
West, Richard, *s* John and Mary West, shoemaker, borne 22th January *c*	9 ,,
Shotten, Alice, *d* Thomas and Frances Shotten, shoemaker, borne 18th January *c*	18 ,,
Browne, Mary, *d* Jeremiah and Isabell Browne, browne 26 December 1659 [no date of Baptism].	
Mackris, Thomas, *s* Thomas and Ann Mackris, shoemaker, borne 14th February *c*	11 Mar.
Fowler, William, *s* Robert and Mary Fowler, glover, borne 4th March *c*	11 ,,
Dales, Faith, *d* John and Ellen Dales, translater, borne 10th February *c*	11 ,,
Francis, John, *s* Thomas and Margaret Francis, felmonger, borne 10th March *s*	18 ,,
Westeby, Edward, *s* William and Sarah Westeby, painter, borne 11th March *c*	18 ,,

[Fol. 37*b*.]

BUBYALLS, 1659.

Riley, Margaret, widdow *b*	6 April
White, Sasanna, wife Thomas White *b*	10 ,,
Sadler, Ann, wife William Sadler *b*	10 ,,
Lill, Margaret, wife Thomas Lill *b*	18 ,,
Greene, William, an infant *b*	26 ,,
Maddison, Henry, glover *b*	29 ,,
Greene, James, a youth *b*	29 ,,
Browne, John, an infant *b*	29 ,,
Burton, Luke, woolen draper *b*	13 May
Vinter, Adam, laborer *b*	18 ,,
Woodthorp, Thomas, an infant *b*	20 ,,
Hamerton, Mary, an infant *b*	28 ,,
Lanes, Pretasie, widdow *b*	8 June
Vinter, William, an infant *b*	20 ,,
Burton, William, an infant *b*	7 July
Goode, James, a little boy *b*	17 ,,
Smith, Elibabeth, widdow *b*	18 ,,
Groome, Dorothy, a yong virgin *b*	30 ,,
Ashley, Gilbert, servant to George Boulton *d*	22 Aug.
Davison, Mrs. Mary, widdow *b*	18 Sept.
Chapman, Elisabeth, a yong virgin *b*	23 ,,
Peares, Ann, wife Ensoby Peares, currier *b*	26 ,,
Smith, Alice, wife John Smith, ironmonger *b*	16 Oct.
Bonner, Joane, wife Richard Bonner, labourer *b*	17 ,,
Stubbs, Mary, *al's.* Freston, spinster *b*	18 ,,
Gresham, Elizabeth, a yong virgin *b*	24 ,,
Pearpoint, Mary, *d* William Pearpoint *b*	3 Nov.
Graves, Samuell, an infant *b*	4 ,,
Attenell, Elisabeth, widdow *b*	10 ,,
Etherington, John, tanner *b*	18 ,,
Chambers, Edward, laborer *b*	22 ,,
Bocock, Mary, wife John Bocock *b*	14 Dec.
Lanes, Mary, wife William Lanes, taylor *b*	15 ,,
Bonner, Susanna, an infant *b*	26 ,,
Sanderson, Jane, a yong virgin *b*	8 Jan.
Chapman, Benjamine, *s* John Chapman *b*	5 ,,
Burr, Edward, dresser of the streets *b*	5 ,,
Madens, Mary, a yong virgin *b*	10 ,,
West, Mary, wife John West *b*	11 ,,

— Harrison, Robert, tanner *b*   12 Jan.
— West, Richard, an infant *b*   18 ,,
— Canter, John, a traveller *b*   10 ,,
— Page, Margaret, wife Thomas Page, currier *b*   18 ,,
— Shotten, Alice, an infant *b*   20 ,,
— Shotten, Frances, wife Thomas Shotten, shoemaker *b*   26 ,,
— Bunting, John *b*   29 ,,
— Gill, Mary, wife John Gill, Shepherd *b*   81 ,,
— Lambe, Elizabeth, wife John Lambe, butcher *b*   9 Feb.
— Hanson, Ann, widdow *b*   18 ,,
— Booock, Mary, an infant *b*   8 Mar.
— Thorp, Thomas, an infant *b*   16 ,,
— Bailey, Thomas, laborer *b*   17 ,,

[Fol. 38*a*.]

BIRTHS AND CHRISTENINGS, 1660.

— Cater, Anthony, *s* Richard and Mary Cater, chandler, borne 27th March *c*   81 ,,
— Simpson, Margaret, *d* William and Alice Simpson, tanner, borne 2th April *c*   24 April
— Holdernes, Elizabeth, *d* John Holderness *c*   25 ,,
— Tayler, Nester, *d* Francis and Grace Tayler, glover, borne 10th April *c*   29 ,,
— Booker, Elizabeth, *d* Thomas Booker, Clerk Minister of Horncastle and Dina his wife borne 24th April *c*   8 May
— Smith, Mary, *d* John and Abigail Smith, borne 21th April *c*   8 ,,
— Hamerton, William, *s* Robert and Ann Hamerton, glover, borne 28 June *c*   4 July
— Stanley, William, *s* William and Ellen Stanley, taylor, borne 16th June *c*   15 ,,
— Buddivant, Thomas, *s* Thomas and Ann Buddivant, laborer, borne 23th June *c*   29 ,,
— Dawson, William, *s* John Dawson, baker, comonly called Lincoln John, and Elizabeth his wife, borne 15th Aug. *c*   19 Aug.
— Vinter, Amy, *d* Arthur and Elizabeth Vinter, tanner, borne 25th August *c*   26 ,,
— Osborne, Mary, *d* John and Mary Osborne, laborer, borne 5th August *c*   2 Sept.
— Howgrave, Robert, *s* Alexander and Elizabeth Howgrave, mercer, borne and *c*   7 ,,
— Gentle, John, *s* Benjamine and Elizabeth Gentle, laborer, borne 15th September *c*   23 ,,
— Tayler, Mary, *d* William and Ann Tayler, tanner, borne 29th Sept. *c*   29 ,,
— Harding, John, *s* John and Bridget Harding, clarke of Horncastle, borne 10th October *c*   28 Oct.
— Bonner, Margaret, *d* William and Elizabeth Bonner, laborer, borne 7th October *c*   21 ,,
— Clapham, Edmund, *s* Ralph and Hellen Clapham, carpenter, borne 2th November *c*   6 Nov.
— Markby, John, *s* John and Elizabeth Markby, butcher, borne 6th November *c*   21 ,,

[Fol. 38*b*.]

— Newman, Susanna, *d* John and Penelope Newman, laborer, borne 2th December *c*   9 Dec.
— Huddleston, Frances, *d* Hamlet Huddleston the Scotch post, and Margaret his wife *c*   26 ,,
— Guising, Francis, *s* James and Mary Guising, mason *c*   27 ,,
— Maultby, Sarah, *d* William and Elizabeth Maultby, laborer *c*   3 Jan.
— Thorp, Ann, *d* Thomas and Elisabeth Thorp, glover *c*   13 ,,

— Graysen, Susanna, *d* Edward and Margaret Graysen, laborer *c*   13 Jan.
— Johnson, Matthew, *s* John and Martha Johnson, glassman *c*   17 Feb.
— Sweete, Elizabeth, *d* Christopher and Ann Sweete, mercer *c*   19 ,,
— Lanes, William, *s* William Lanes, taylor *c*   24 ,,
— Johnson, Mary, *d* Roger and Grace Johnson, laborer, *c*   10 Mar.
— Drury, Mary, *d* John and Thudory Drury, barbour *c*   10 ,,

MARRIAGES, 1659 AND 1660.   [1659]

— Simpson, John }
— Newman, Mary } *m*   1 Sept.

— Bilsby, Thomas }
— Walker, Margaret } *m*   27 ,,

— White, Thomas }
— Lamb, Bridget } *m*   13 Oct.

   [1660]

— Bowering, William }
— Elsdon, Ann } *m*   6 Nov.

— Bonner, Richard }
— Pinder, Susanna } *m*   13 ,,

— Osborne, John }
— Gray, Ann } *m*   20 Dec.

— Shepherd, Walter }
— Boulton, Luce } *m* by Mr. Martin Bennet   11 Jan.

   [Fol. 39a.]

BURIALLS, 1660.
— Benton, Thomas, yeoman *b*   1 April
— Shotten, Thomas, labourer *b*   25 ,,
— Hill, Gabriell, an infant *b*   2 May
— Stubbs, Thomas, an infant *b*   8 ,,
— Lanes, Nathaniell, adolescens *b*   15 ,,
— Milner, Ellen, widdow *b*   17 ,,
— Shotten, Susanna, wife Edward Shotten *b*   26 ,,
— Greene, Thomas, Clerk, Minister of Ingoldmells *b*   16 June
— Vinter, Elizabeth, wife John Vinter *b*   20 ,,
— Tinker, Benjamine, an infant *b*   24 ,,
— Nelson, Eustace, translater *b*   2 July
— Simpson, Margaret, an infant *b*   18 ,,
— Joyes, Frances, wife William Joyes *b*   19 ,,
— Bowering, Ann, wife William Bowering *b*   1 Aug.
— Lee, Dynah, wife Henry Lee *b*   23 ,,
— Davison, John, Gent. *b*   24 ,,
— Beswick, Joyes, spinster *b*   29 ,,
— Saddler, William, labourer *b*   12 Sept.
— Cater, Anthony, an infant *b*   12 ,,
— Chambers, Mary, widdow *b*   23 Oct.
— Lanes, Elizabeth, an infant *b*   30 ,,
— Mackris, Thomas, an infant *b*   5 Nov.
— Parrish, Mary, an infant *b*   5 ,,
— Tayler, Sarah, an infant *b*   8 Dec.
Tayler, Ellen, widdow *b*   13 ,,
— Daunse, Elizabeth, wife George Daunse *b*   17 ,,
— Lanes, Margaret, widdow *b*   25 ,,
— Burch, Elizabeth, spinster *b*   12 Jan.
— Benson, Richard, yeoman *b*   15 ,,
Smith, Robert, butcher *b*   30 ,,
— Atkin, Mary, an infant *b*   3 Feb.
— Freston, Abigail, wife Valentine Freston *b*   4 ,,
— Wright, John, adolescens *b*   25 ,,
— Thorpp, Ann, an infant *b*   25 ,,
— Hutchinson, Bridget, wife John Hutchinson, shoemaker *b*   15 Mar.

CHRISTENINGS, 1661.

Graves, Elizabeth, *d* Ralph and Lidia Graves, sadler *c* — 15 April
Tinker, Mary, *d* Thomas and Anne Tinker, taylor *c* — 16 ,,
Martin, Katherine, *d* John and Elizabeth Martin *c* — 16 ,,
Markby, Elizabeth, *d* of Hastens and Margaret Markby, butcher *c* — 18 May
Elston, Mary, *d* George and Ellen Elston, tayler *c* — 17 ,,
Dales, John, *s* John and Ellen Dales, translater *c* — 19 ,,
Mellers, Richard, *s* Richard and Ann Mellers *c* — 80 ,,
Castledine, Penelope, *d* Ralph and Elizabeth Castledine, labourer *c* — 12 June

[Fol. 89*b*.]

Goode, Elizabeth, *d* Thomas and Mary Goode, taylor, borne 4th June *c* — 18 ,,
Ayscough, Thomas, *s* Francis and Margaret Ayscough, Apothecary *c* — 11 ,,
Page, Susanna, *d* Richard and Susanna Page, currier *c* — 80 ,,
Greene, James, *s* Robert and Sarah Greene, laborer *c* — 7 July
Joyes, Susanna, *d* William and Susanna Joyes, labourer *c* — 4 Aug.
Cater, Elizabeth, *d* Richard and Mary Cater, chandler *c* — 1 Sept.
Beighton, Margaret, *d* William and Ann Beighton, laborer *c* — 5 ,,
Parker, William, *s* Edward Parker, taylor *c* — 5 ,,
Dales, Thomas, *s* Nicholas and Jane Dales, taylor *c* — 21 ,,
West, William, *s* John West, shoemaker *c* — 22 ,,
Hamerton, Margaret, *d* Samuel and Susanna Hamerton, tanner *c* — 22 ,,
Mackris, Elizabeth, *d* Thomas and Ann Mackris *c* — 6 Oct.
Harding, Samuell, *s* Frances and Lidia Harding, shoemaker *c* — 12 ,,
Pell, Dorothy, *d* James and Marah Pell, ironmonger *c* — 18 ,,
Hamerton, Samuell, *s* Robert and Ann Hamerton, glover *c* — 27 ,,
Barnard, Thomas, *s* Thomas and Ann Barnard, butcher *c* — 8 Nov.
Shepherd, John, *s* Walter and Luce Shepherd, shoemaker *c* — 12 ,,
Bowering, William, *s* William and Anne Bowering, coop[er] *c* — 8 Dec.
Hancock, William, *s* John and Alice Hancock *c* — 16 ,,

[Fol. 40*a*.]

Kerke, Mary, *d* William and Mary Kerke, tinker *c* — 29 ,,
Smith, Sarah, *d* William Smith, mason *c* — 12 Jan,
Frances, Thomas, *s* Thomas and Frances Smith, felmonger *c* — 20 ,,
Guising, Frances, *d* George and Elizabéth Guising, mercer, borne 14th January *c* — 21 ,,
Osborne, William, *s* John and Ann Osborne, weaver *c* — 9 Mar.
Browne, Bridget, *d* Jeremiah and Isabel Browne, whitesmith *c* — 25 Feb.
Howgrave, George, *s* Alexander and Elizabeth Howgrave, mercer *c* — 24 Mar.

[Note]—Here endeth Christenings, 1661.

MARRIAGES, 1661.

Hancock, John } *m* — 15 April
Fisher, Alice }
Freston, Valentine } *m* — 80 ,,
Betts, Alice }
Perkins, Thomas } *m* — 7 May
Raithby, Alice }
Clarke, Richard } *m* — 28 ,,
Benton, Joane }
Burch, Thomas } *m* — 28 ,,
Mawer, Rosamond }
Bankes, John } *m* — 6 Oct.
Shepherd, Elizabeth }

-Butler, Joseph } *m* [but no date of marriage].
-Vrye, Elizabeth }

BURYALLS, 1661.

- Gresham, Elizabeth, widdow *b*	15 April
Barnay, Robert, of Miningsby *b*	25 ,,
- Clay, John, *al's* Stanforth, tanner *b*	2 May
Welsher, John, tanner *b*	10 ,,
Howgrave, Robert, an infant *b*	20 ,,
White, Mary, spinster *b*	26 June
Banes, Ann, spinster *b*	4 July
Woodthorp, Ann, spinster *b*	10 ,,
Winter, Symon, cooper *b*	15 ,,
Cottam, Thomas, an infant *b*	27 ,,
Thompson, Mary, spinster *b*	9 Aug.
Huddleston, Frances, an infant *b*	13 ,,
Dodkin, Elizabeth, wife Vincent Dodkin *b*	16 ,,
Webster, Elizabeth, spinster *b*	19 ,,
Chester, Mary, wife William Chester *b*	6 Sept.
Attenell, Alice, wife John Attenell *b*	23 ,,
Bonner, Isabel, spinster *b*	2 Oct.
Clark, William, yeoman *b*	9 ,,
Harding, Samuel, an infant *b*	13 ,,
Stanforth, Mary, widdow *b*	17 ,,
Mackris, Ann, wife Thomas Mackris *b*	30 ,,
Winter, Elizabeth, widdow *b*	12 Nov.
Wood, Robert, an infant *b*	26 ,,

[Fol. 40*b*.]

Johnson, Martin, tanner *b*	6 Dec.
Hancock, William, an infant *b*	19 ,,
Fowler, Mary, an infant *b*	27 ,,
Fowler, William, an infant *b*	11 Jan.
Hamerton, Samuell, an infant *b*	11 ,,
Bonner, William, tanner *b*	13 ,,
Wright, Thomas, shoemaker *b*	10 Feb.
Markby, Elizabeth, an infant *b*	19 ,,
Lambert, John, butcher *b*	28 ,,
Daunce, Ellen, an infant *b*	21 ,,
Graves, Elizabeth, an infant *b*	8 Mar.
Wade, William, adolescence *b*	12 ,,
Webster, John, an infant *b*	15 ,,
Ayscough, Thomas, an infant *b*	20 ,,

[Note]—Here endeth Buryalls, 1661.

CHRISTENINGS, 1662.

Perkins, Mary, *d* Thomas and Alice Perkins *c*	27 ,,
Clapham, Thomas, *s* Ralph and Ellen Clapham *c*	31 ,,
Tayler, Thomas, *s* Robert and Elizabeth Tayler, felmonger *c*	31 ,,
Bocock, Luce, *d* John and Ann Bocock, labourer *c*	27 April
Carr, Mary, *d* Thomas and Mary Carr, shoemaker *c*	19 May
Blow, Godfrey, *s* William and Ann Blow, barbour *c*	25 ,,
Dawson, William, *s* Thomas and Magdalen Dawson, laborer *c*	25 ,,
Bonner, Ustace, *s* Richard and Susanna Bonner *c*	1 June
Thorp, Susanna, *d* Thomas and Elizabeth Thorp, felmonger *c*	22 ,,
Butler, Elizabeth, *d* Mr. John Butler and Elizabeth his wife *c*	24 ,,
Fisher, Christo[pher], *s* Christopher and Elizabeth Fisher, whitesmith *c*	25 ,,
Bankes, John, *s* John and Elizabeth Bankes, miller *c*	31 Aug.
Castledine, Elizabeth, *d* Ralph Castledine, yeoman *c*	4 Sept.
Parrish, Richard, *s* John and Ellen Parrish, taylor *c*	10 ,,

[Fol. 41a.]

Newman, Susanna, d John and Penelope Newman, labourer c	21 Sept.
Huddleston, Sarah, d Hamlet and Mary Huddleston, labourer c	4 Oct.
Westeby, William, s William and Sarah Westeby, painter c	5 ,,
Paddison, Thomas, s —— and —— Paddison of —— in the county of York c	2 Nov.
Ayscough, Francis, s Francis and Margaret Ayscough, Apothecarie c	27 ,,
Smith, Thomas, s Thomas and Elizabeth Smith c	7 Dec.
Batty, Jane, d Francis and Elizabeth Batty, barbour c	9 ,,
Martin, Elizabeth, d John and Elizabeth Martin c	9 Jan.
Johnson, Mary, d William and Ann Johnson, shoemaker c	10 ,,
Bonner, William, s William and Elizabeth Bonner, labourer c	8 Feb.
Eldred, Elizabeth, d John and Lidia Eldred c	8 ,,
Tayler, Christopher, s William and Ann Tayler, tanner c	12 ,,
Gibson, Susanna, d Joseph and Susanna Gibson, cooper c	1 Mar.
Hamerton, Mary, d John and Lydia Hamerton, the yonger, tanner c	24 ,,
Goode, Mary, d Thomas and Mary Goode c	24 ,,

MARRIAGES, 1662.

Eldred, John } m Dawson, Lydia }	18 May
Gibbon, John } m Crastes, Elisabeth }	22 ,,
Onseman, William } m Minting, Elizabeth }	20 ,,
Gibson, Joshua } m Leake, Susanna }	10 July
Eyre, Alexander } m Cammell, Mary }	7 Aug.
Onseman, Robert } m Cammell, Elisabeth }	15 Oct.
Willyamson, Robert } m Etherington, Joane }	1 Nov.
Browne, Thomas } m Hardy, Ann }	27 ,,
Wright, John } m Clarke, Margaret }	22 Jan.

BURYALLS, 1662.

Maidens, Edward, an infant b	29 Mar.
Gillam, Jane, wife Thomas Gillam b	31 ,,
Perkins, Mary, an infant b	4 April
Moweray, Susanna, widow b	7 ,,
Wallis, Alice, widow b	17 ,,
Newman, Susanna, an infant b	8 May
Tayler, Elizabeth, spinster b	9 ,,
Cater, Richard, an infant b	11 ,,
Watson, William, labourer b	4 June

[Fol. 41b.]

Dales, John, an infant b	9 ,,
Smithan, Thomas, an infant b	9 ,,
Tayler, Thomas, an infant b	9 ,,
Tayler, Thomas, butcher b	5 July
Clapham, Thomas, an infant b	10 ,,
Tayler, Ann, widow b	10 Aug.
Richardson, Mary, wife John Richardson b	15 ,,
Pell, Charles, an infant b	27 Sept.
Paddison, Thomas, an infant b	3 Nov.
Johnson, Mary, an infant b	4 ,,

Surflet, Ann, widow *b*	7 Nov.
Smith, John, chairmaker *b*	9 „
Ayscough, Francis, an infant *b*	29 „
Stubbs, Peter the yonger, glaisier *b*	9 Dec.
Markby, Elizabeth, spinster *b*	26 „
Maidens, Thomas, an infant *b*	4 Jan.
Osborn, John the elder, labourer *b*	28 „
Johnson, Mary, an infant *b*	28 „
Huddleston, Robert, an infant *b*	28 Mar.

CHRISTENINGS, 1663.

Markby, George, *s* Hasten and Ann Markby, butcher *c*	3 April
Shepherd, Walter, *s* Walter and Luce Shepherd, shoemaker *c*	19 „
Groome, Thomas, bastard childe of Elizabeth Groome and putative of Thomas Woodthorp, tanner *c*	20 „
Storry, Robert, *s* John and Elizabeth Storry, wollen draper *c*	2 June
Gurness, William, *s* James and Mary Gurness *c*	7 „
Eyre, Thomas, *s* Alexander and Mary Eyre *c*	14 „
Gentle, Elizabeth, *d* Benam and Elizabeth Gentle *c*	23 May
Browne, George, *s* Thomas and Ann Browne *c*	19 June
Clapham, Joseph, *s* Ralph and Ellen Clapham *c*	21 „
Cockborne, John, *s* George and Elizabeth Cockborne *c*	9 July
Hancock, Alice, *s* John and Alice Hancock *c*	12 „
Page, Thomas, *s* Thomas and Elizabeth Page *c*	24 „

[Fol. 42*a*.]

Perkins, Ann, *d* Thomas and Alice Perkins *c*	27 „
Houldernes, Mary, *d* John and Frances Houldernes *c*	30 Aug.
Hareby, William, *s* William and Dorothy Hareby *c*	6 Sept.
Gibbon, John, *s* John and Elizabeth Gibbon *c*	17 „
Greenfield, Hanna, *d* Gervas and Jane Greenfield *c*	1 Oct.
Howgrave, Elizabeth, *d* Alexander and Elizabeth Howgrave, mercer *c*	11 „
Cater, Mary, *d* Richard and Mary Cater, chandler *c*	14 „
Browne, Richard, *s* Richard and Ann Browne, shoemaker *c*	2 „
Tinker, Richard, *s* Thomas and Ann Tinker, taylor *c*	5 „
Johnson, John, *s* John and Martha Johnson, glasman *c*	8 „
Butler, Samuell, *s* Joseph and Elizabeth Butler *c*	10 Nov.
Dales, Mary, *d* John and Ellen Dales *c*	29 „
West, Elizabeth, *d* John West, shoemaker *c*	28 Dec.
Drury, John, *s* John Drury, barbour *c*	29 „
Osborn, Ann, *d* John Osborn, weaver *c*	30 „
Plumpton, Thomas, *s* George Plumpton, basket maker *c*	30 „
Hayns, Jane, *d* Charles Hayns, taylour *c*	7 Jan.
Newman, Penelope, *d* John Newman, labourer *c*	27 „
Fowler, George, *s* Robert and Mary Fowler *c*	14 Feb.
Ayscough, Edward, *s* Francis Ayscough, Apothecary *c*	23 „
Graves, Lidia, *d* Ralph and Lidia Graves, sadler *c*	28 „
Cottam, William, *s* John and Jane Cottam, baker *c*	1 Mar.
Hamerton, Thomas, *s* Thomas and Mary Hamerton, tanner *c*	28 „

[Fol. 42*b*.]

MARRIAGES, 1663.

Darby, John Hollingworth, Ellen } *m*	7 May
Marshall, Thomas Smith, Jane } *m*	15 „
Dodkin, Vincent Jeffrey, Elizabeth } *m*	25 June
Gunwell, Jeffrey, Clerke Neave, Mrs. Ann } *m*	20 Aug.

Dixon, William	*m*	
Nicholls, Mary		8 Oct.
Haward, Danyell	*m*	
Hill, Ann		21 Jan.
Shallock, Thomas	*m*	
Dennys, Mary		2 Feb.

BURIALLS, 1663.

Guising, William, mercer *b*	10 April
Wells, Robert, tanner, a yong man *b*	10 ,,
Sanderson, John, a stranger *b*	17 ,,
Merriwether, Elizabeth, spinster *b*	21 ,,
Scamblesby, Elizabeth, spinster *b*	21 ,,
Groome, Thomas, bastard childe of Elizabeth Groome *b*	22 ,,
Thompson, Catherine, widow *b*	22 ,,
Nelsey, William, a yong man *b*	4 May
Hamerton, Mary, an infant *b*	4 ,,
Daunse, George, glover *b*	6 ,,
Peares, Stephen, an infant *b*	6 ,,
Eyre, Thomas, an infant *b*	19 ,,
Hutchinson, Ann, wife Robert Hutchinson *b*	21 ,,
Clapham, Ellen, wife Ralph Clapham *b*	29 ,,
Hutchinson, Elizabeth, an infant *b*	30 ,,
Browne, George, an infant *b*	1 July
Lill, Thomas, taylour *b*	30 ,,
Smith, Jeremiah, a yong youth *b*	31 ,,
Perkins, Ann, an infant *b*	9 Aug.
Littlebury, Mary, wife Thomas Littlebury *b*	19 ,,
Gibbon, John, an infant *b*	20 Sept.
Harris, John, labourer *b*	25 ,,
Lawrence, John, *al's* Attenell *b*	2 Oct.
Greenfield, Hanna, an infant *b*	4 ,,
Hutchinson, Margaret, wife John Hutchinson *b*	18 ,,
Haward, Mary, wife Danyell Haward *b*	4 Nov.
Howgrave, Elizabeth, an infant *b*	30 Dec.
Haynes, Jane, an infant *b*	20 ,,
Johnson, Elizabeth, spinster *b*	20 Jan.
Cammell, Margaret, wife Nicholas Cammell *b*	4 Feb.

[Fol. 43a.]

CHRISTENINGS, 1664.

Eldred, Lydia, *d* John and Lydia Eldred, baker *c*	27 Mar.
Hamerton, Samuell, *s* Samuell and Susanna Hamerton *c*	19 April
Hamerton, Mary, *d* John and Lidia Hamerton, jun., tanner *c*	26 ,,
Elston, Ann, *d* George and Ellen Elston, taylor *c*	8 May
Tayler, Elizabeth, *d* Robert and Elizabeth Tayler, glover *c*	29 ,,
Bowering, Jone, *d* William and Ann Bowering, cooper *c*	31 ,,
Dodkin, George, *s* Vincent and Elizabeth Dodkin *c*	13 June
Blow, Elizabeth, *d* William and Ann Blow, barbour *c*	13 ,,
Simpson, Bridget, *d* William and Alice Simpson, tanner *c*	19 ,,
Dixon, Thomas, *s* William and Mary Dixon, carpenter *c*	26 ,,
Castledine, Bridget, *d* Ralph and Elizabeth Castledine *c*	26 ,,
Lanes, Elizabeth, *d* William and Sarah Lanes *c*	12 July
Addison, Charles, *s* Charles and Mary Addison, miller *c*	21 Aug.
Chester, Sarah, *d* William and Mary Chester, gardiner *c*	26 ,,
White, Bridget, *d* Thomas and Bridget White, weaver *c*	18 Sept.
Burton, Ellen, *d* Thomas and Ann Burton, labourer *c*	28 ,,
Smith, William, *s* William and Margaret Smith, mason *c*	6 Oct.
Kerk, William, *s* William and Mary Kerk, tinker *c*	9 ,,
Freston, Thomas, *s* Thomas and Grace Freston, Gent. *c*	18 ,,
Garness, Priscilla, *d* of James and Mary Garness, mason *c*	4 Nov.

Haward, Ellenor, *d* Danyell and Ann Haward *c*   4 Dec.
Davison, Grace, *d* Thomas and Magdalen Davison, labourer *c*   11 „
Peares, Ann, *d* Ensoby and Mary Peares *c*   11 „
Vrye, Isabell, *d* Thomas and Katherine Vrye, mercer *c*   13 „
Vinter, Richard, *s* John and Mary Vinter, glover *c*   26 „
Browne, Jeremiah, *s* Jeremiah and Isabell Browne, whitesmith *c*   27 „
Story, Elizabeth, *d* John and Elizabeth Story, woollen draper   30 „
Gibbon, Joseph, *s* John and Elizabeth Gibbon, mason *c*   7 Jan.
[Fol. 43*b*.]
Culyer, Ann, *d* and bastard of Elizabeth Culyer *c*   25 „
Tharrold, Elizabeth, *d* Paul and Alice Tharrold *c*   26 „
Carr, Thomas, *s* Thomas and Mary Carr, shoemaker *c*   26 Feb.
Littlebury, Mary, *d* Thomas and Grace Littlebury *c*   28 „
Markby, William, *s* Hastens and Ann Markby *c*   1 Mar.
Francis, Robert, *s* Thomas and Margaret Francis, glover *c*   5 „
Dawson, Stephen, *s* Joshua and Ann Dawson, tanner *c*   23 „

MARRIAGES, 1664.

Giliam, Thomas ⎱ *m*   21 April
Lambe, Elizabeth ⎰
Hamerton, Thomas ⎱ *m*   28 „
Tayler, Jane ⎰
Goisborrow, William ⎱ *m*   1 May
Benton, Elizabeth ⎰
Stevenson, Robert ⎱ *m*   3 June
Castledine, Elizabeth ⎰
Bird, John ⎱ *m*   2 Aug.
Mawer, Ann ⎰
Burton, Thomas ⎱ *m*   8 Sept.
Spendley, Ann ⎰
Markby, William ⎱ *m*   8 Nov.
Tayler, Ann ⎰
Maughan, John ⎱ *m* wth. a lycense   29 „
Dennys, Penelope ⎰

BURIALLS, 1664.

Hamerton, Thomas, an infant *b*   26 Mar.
Hamerton, Mary, wife of Thomas Hamerton, mother of the said infant *b*   27 „
Freston, Valentine, laborer *b*   15 April
Meriwether, Richard, glover *b*   22 „
Williman, Gilbert, felmonger *b*   12 May
Smith, John, *s* of Mr. Stephen Smith *b*   6 June
Wombwell, Amy, wife Lawrence Wombell *b*   28 „
Guising, George, *s* George Guising, mercer *b*   1 July
Peak, Thomas, a yong youth *b*   4 „
Vinter, Richard, an infant *b*   31 „
Hutchinson, John, laborer *b*   10 Aug.
Tayler, Elizabeth, an infant *b*   16 „
Davison, Benjamine *b*   1 Sept.
Francis, Ann, wife Hermon Francis *b*   7 Oct.
Burton, Ellen, an infant *b*   8 „
Barnard, Robert, laborer *b*   23 „
Holdernes, Mary, an infant *b*   24 „
Freston, Thomas, *s* Thomas Freston, Gent. *b*   2 Nov.
Garnes, Priscilla, an infant *b*   4 „
Marley, Ann, widdow *b*   6 „
Rawson, William, a yong youth *b*   2 Jan.
Vinter, Richard, an infant *b*   6 „
Portes, Dorothy, wife of George Portes *b*   11 „
Ashton, Sarah, widdow *b*   14 „

—Let, Henry, who lived of collection b .... 17 Jan.
—Lyell, William, who lived the like b .... 24 ,,
— Burton, Ellen, an infant b .... 29 ,,

[Fol. 44a.]

~ Culyer, Ann, the bastard childe of Elizabeth Culyer b .... 3 Feb.
—Vrye, Isabel, an infant b .... 6 ,,
—Moyser, Ann, spinster b .... 15 ,,
—Bunting, Elizabeth, widdow b .... 7 Mar.

CHRISTENINGS, 1665.

—Westeby, Damaris, d William and Sarah Westeby c .... 26 ,,
—Golsborrow, Mary, d William and Elizabeth Golsborrow c .... 28 ,,
—Stevenson, Ann, d Robert and Elizabeth Stevenson c .... 28 ,,
—Bonner, Ann, d William and Elizabeth Bonner c .... 2 April
—Darby, John, s John and Ellen c .... 9 ,,
—Perkins, Elizabeth, d Thomas and Alice Perkins c .... 9 ,,
—Howgrave, Mary, d Alexander and Elizabeth Howgrave c .... 18 ,,
—Maultby, Ann, d William and Elizabeth Maultby c .... 30 ,,
—Gibson, Thomas, s Joseph and Susanna Gibson c .... 5 May
—Enderby, William, s William and Susanna c .... 7 ,,
—Tayler, Robert, s William and Ann Tayler, tanner c .... 21 ,,
—Smith, Ann, d John and Margaret Smith, ironmonger c .... 30 ,,
— Bocock, William, s John and Mary Bocock c .... 11 June
· Wright, Elizabeth, d George and Elizabeth Wright the yonger c .... 11 ,,
—Martindale, Mary, d Robert and Mary Martindale c .... 12 ,,
—Empson, Mary, d Thomas and Susanna Empson, tanner c .... 13 ,,
—Huddleston, Bridget, d Hamlet and Margaret Huddleston c .... 18 ,,
· Fowler, Isaac, s Robert and Mary Fowler c .... 25 ,,
—Eldred, Sarah, d John and Lidia Eldred c .... 2 July
— Lathorp, John, s William and Grace Lathorp c .... 21 ,,
—Guising, George, s George and Elizabeth c .... 8 Aug.
— Goude, Thomas, s Thomas and Mary Goude c .... 4 Sept.
— Cockbourne, Elizabeth, d George and Elizabeth Cockbourne c . 5 ,,

[Fol. 44b.]

—Dixon, Charles, s William and Mary Dixon c .... 10 ,,
—Gillam, Thomas, s Thomas and Elizabeth Gillam c .... 1 Oct.
— Tayler, John, s Robert and Elizabeth Tayler c .... 8 ,,
—Holdernes, John, s John and Frances Holdernes c .... 8 ,,
—Burton, Thomas, s William and Ann Burton c .... 8 ,,
—Browne, Joseph, s Richard and Ann Browne c .... 8 Nov.
· Grove, John, s Augustine and Frances Grove c .... 14 ,,
· Gurness, Mary, d James and Mary Gurness c .... 14 ,,
— Bird, Mary, d John and Ann Bird c .... 17 ,,
—Barnard, Martha, d Thomas and Ann Barnard c .... 24 ,,
· Markby, John, s William and Ann Markby c .... 28 ,,
< Haward, Thomas, s Danyell and Ann Haward c .... 24 Dec.
—Tayler, Mary, d William and Ann Tayler c .... 26 ,,
—Tinker, Mary, d Thomas and Ann Tinker c .... 26 ,,
—Cater, Susanna, d Richard and Mary Cater c .... 27 ,,
· Shepherd, John, s Walter and Luce Shepherd c .... 27 ,,
—Tharrold, Gertrude, d John and Gartree Tharrold c .... 28 ,,
—Chester, Francis, d William and Mary Chester c .... 10 Jan.
—Page, John, s Thomas and Elizabeth Page c .... 17 ,,
—Parker, Elizabeth, d William and Mary Parker c .... 17 ,,
—Thorp, Jane, d Thomas and Elizabeth Thorp c .... 4 Feb.
—Hancock, Stephen, s John and Alice Hancock c .... 20 ,,
— Gentle, Jane, d Benjamine and Elizabeth Gentle c .... 21 ,,
—Shotten, Thomas, s Thomas and —— Shotten c .... 4 Mar.
— Littlebury, Thomas, s Thomas and Grace Littlebury c .... 8 ,,
— Clapham, Ralph, s Ralph and Mary Clapham c .... 11 ,,

Crosby { John, Thomas, *ss* Richard and ——— Crosby *c*		11 Mar.
Looking, John, *s* Gilbert and Bridget Looking *c* [Fol. 45*a*.]		11 ,,

MARRIAGES, 1665.

Marr, Robert Cottam, Elisabeth } *m*		4 April
Freeman, George Tayler, Isabell } *m*		6 ,,
Whitesmith, Edward Salmon, Susanna } *m*		11 ,,
Looking, Gilbert Poutherill, Bridgett } *m*		28 May
Minting, Richard Shortt, Elizabeth } *m*		1 June
Broughton, John Clarke, Ann } *m*		6 ,,
Joanes, Symon Smith, Margaret } *m*		1 Aug.
George, Robert Castledine, Frances } *m*		8 Feb.

BURIALLS, 1665.

Joanes, Mary, wife of Symon Joanes *b*	8 May
Lindley, Mary, widdow *b*	14 ,,
Castledine, Bridget, an infant *b*	14 ,,
Yates, Elizabeth, widdow *b*	16 ,,
Gibbon, Joseph, an infant *b*	4 June
Cottam, William, an infant *b*	4 ,,
Bonner, Elizabeth, an infant *b*	5 ,,
Buckingham, George, a youth and a stranger *b*	6 ,,
Smith, Margaret, wife John Smith, ironmonger *b*	18 ,,
Block, John, a yong youth *b*	4 July
Shepherd, John, an infant *b*	11 ,,
Willyamson, Roger, a youth slane in a tanner bark mill *b*	23 ,,
Goulsborrow, William, labourer *b*	6 Aug.
Guising, George, an infant *b*	17 ,,
Castledine, Elizabeth, wife Ralph Castledine *b*	28 ,,
Boulton, Ellen, wife George Boulton *b*	31 ,,
Goulde, Thomas, an infant *b*	5 Sept.
Hall, Thomas, cordwiner *b*	7 ,,
Johnson, John, butcher *b*	27 ,,
Hansard, Frances, widdow *b*	12 Oct.
Boocock, William, an infant *b*	19 ,,
Gurness, Mary, an infant *b*	29 Nov.
Almaine, Thomas, an infant *b*	28 Dec.
Tharrold, Gartree, wife John Tharrold *b*	28 ,,
Dodkin, George, an infant *b*	30 ,,
Hamerton, Thomas, felmonger *b*	16 Jan.
Markby, John, an infant *b*	26 ,,
Fisher, Christopher, whitesmith *b*	27 ,,
Burton, Mary, a yong virgin *b*	2 Feb.
Elston, Mary, an infant *b*	22 ,,
Chamberlane, Mary, wife John Chamberlane *b*	2 Mar.
Smith, John, tanner *b*	8 ,,
Tayler, John, an infant *b*	8 ,,
Tothby, Mary, wife Robert Tothby *b*	9 ,,
Crosby, John, an infant *b*	12 ,,
Looking, John, an infant *b*	13 ,,
Crosby, Thomas, an infant *b*	14 ,,

Bowering, William, cooper *b* .... 24 Mar.

[Fol. 45*b*.]

CHRISTENINGS, 1666.

- Browne, Thomas, *s* Jeremiah and Isabell Browne *c* ...... 25 „
- Blow, William, *s* William and Ann Blow *c* .... 28 „
- Freeman, Thomas, *s* George and Isabell Freeman *c* ...... 31 „
- Dales, John, *s* John and Hellen Dales *c* .... 1 April
- Simpson, Ann, *d* William and Alice Simpson *c* .... 22 „
- Broughton, Isabell, *d* John and Ann Broughton *c* ...... 22 „
- Gibbon, Henry, *s* John and Elizabeth Gibbon *c* .... 6 May
- Bonner, Thomas, *s* William and Elizabeth Bonner *c* .... 13 „
- Fisher, Thomas, *s* Christopher Fisher, whitesmith, now
    deceased, and ——— his wife now widdow *c* .... 22 „
- Hamerton, Lidia, *d* John and Lidia Hamerton *c* .... 4 June
  Brough, Mary, *d* Robert Brough and Margaret his wife being
    travellers *c* .... 6 „
- Plumpton, Edward, *s* George and Ann Plumpton *c* ...... 24 „
- Haynes, John, *s* Charles and Ellen Haynes *c* .... 1 July
  Dawson, Elizabeth, *d* Thomas and Magdalen Dawson *c* .. 1 „
- Marley, Jonathan, *s* Joshua and Mary Marley *c* .... 1 „
- Enderby, Rose, *d* Samuel and Rose Enderby *c* .... 1 „
- Minting, Katherine, *d* Richard and Elizabeth Minting *c* .. 17 „
- Butler, John, *s* Joseph and Elizabeth Butler *c* .... 19 „
- Freston, Francis, *s* Thomas and Grace Freston, Gent. *c* .. 24 „
- Wright, George, *s* George and Elizabeth Wright *c* ...... 8 Aug.
- Marr, Amye, *d* Robert and Elizabeth Marr *c* .... 16 „
- Osborne, John, *s* John and Ann Osborne *c* .... 2 Sept.
- Tharrold, Ellenor, *d* Paul and Alice Tharrold *c* ...... 2 „
- West, Martha, *d* John and Ann West *c* .... 16 „
- Goude, Thomas, *s* Thomas and Mary Goude *c* .... 2 Oct.
- Atkinson, Mary, *d* Edward and Elizabeth Atkinson *c* .... 5 „
- Dowse, Margaret, the bastard childe of Margaret Dowse and
    putative of Bryan Westland *c* .... 7 „

[Fol. 46*a*.]

- Lathorp, Elizabeth, *d* William and Grace Lathorp *c* .... 12 „
- Williman, Mary, *d* Gilbert and Mary Williman *c* ...... 6 Nov.
- Ayscough, Anne, *d* Thomas and Mary Ayscough *c* ...... 20 „
- Marley, Samuell, *s* Jonathan and Ann Marley *c* .... 2 Dec.
- Simson, Mathew, *s* John and Elizabeth Simson *c* ...... 26 „
- Tottrell, Agnes, *d* Edward and Elizabeth Tottrell *c* .... 25 Nov.
- Adison, Mary, *d* Charles and Mary Adison *c* .... 6 Jan.
- Tayler, Elin, *d* Robert and Elin Tayler *c* .... 9 „
- Dickson, Elizabeth, *d* Willyam and Mary Dickson *c* .... 10 „
  Martindale, Christopher, *s* Robert and Mary Martindale *c* .. 13 „
- Fouller, Mary, *d* Robert and Mary Fouller *c* .... 20 „
- West, Alse, *d* Nathanyell and Elizabeth West *c* ...... 20 „
- Kerk, William, *s* William and Mary Kerk *c* .... 27 „
- Francis, Richard, *s* Herman and Elizabeth Francis *c* .... 17 Feb.
- Serby, Martha, *d* George and Martha Serby *c* .... 21 „
- Garnish, Elizabeth, *d* James and Mary Garnish *c* ...... 24 „
- Dodkin, Vincent, *s* Vincent and Elizabeth Dodkin *c* .... 24 „
- Markby, Margaret, *d* Hastens and Ann Markby *c* ...... 5 Mar.

MARRIAGES, 1666.

- Stubbe, Thomas }
- Douse, Margaret } *m* .... 11 June
- Cooke, Richard }
- Gibson, Margery } *m* .... 14 „
- Simson, John }
- Hardy, Elizabeth } *m* .... 23 Aug.

- Bowring, George	} m	15 Nov.
- Forman, Susanna		
- Goose, Nathanyall	} m with a licence	17 Dec.
- Harding, Bridget		
- Tunstall, Edmund	} m with a licence	14 Feb.
- Guysing, Milldred		

[Fol. 46b.]

BURIALLS, 1666.

White, Bridget, an infant b	27 Mar.
Houier, Isaack, an infant b	29 ,,
Wright, George, ye elder b	6 April
Thorp, Jane, an infant b	10 ,,
Freeman, Thomas, an infant b	9 ,,
Maultby, Margaret, spinster b	17 ,,
Nelsey, John, a youth b	3 May
Simson, Mary, wife John Simson b	19 ,,
Elston, Ellen, wife George Elston b	20 ,,
Hamerton, Lidia, wife John Hamerton b	4 June
Plumton, Edward, an infant b	26 ,,
Groume, George, a tanner b	13 July
Butler, John, an infant b	30 ,,
Johnson, John, glasman b	8 Aug.
Bonner, Ann, an infant b	9 ,,
Cookburn, Elizabeth, an infant b	10 ,,
Parker, William, an infant b	15 Sept.
Coupland, George b	7 Oct.
Francis, Robert, an infant b	24 ,,
Cooke, Ann, widdow b	8 Nov.
Lathorop, Elizabeth, an infant b	11 ,,
Atkingson, Elizabeth, an infant b	19 ,,
Tunstall, Jane, wife Edmund Tunstall b	21 ,,
Harding, John, Parish Clerke* b	3 Dec.
Pogson, Joane, widdow b	8 ,,
Tayler, Lawrence b	31 ,,
Wells, Nicholas b	4 Jan.
Baley, Elizabeth b	6 ,,
Dixon, Samuell b	7 ,,
Barron, Elizabeth, wife William Barron b	18 ,,
Bradley, Katherin, widdow b	24 ,,
Dance, Steaven b	6 Feb.
Tayler, Elizabeth, ye bastard child of Joyes Tayler b	10 ,,
Dixon, Mary, wife William Dixon b	10 ,,
Francis, Richard, an infant b	18 ,,
Pogson, Samuell b	19 ,,
Freston, Francis, an infant b	19 ,,
Nickools, Elizabeth, wife Thomas Nickools b	24 ,,
Dodkin, Vincent, an infant b	28 ,,
Parrish, Elizabeth, an infant b	28 ,,
Grove, Elizabeth b	5 Mar.
Kerk, William, an infant b	9 ,,

[Fol. 47a.]

Hamerton, Robert, tanner b	12 ,,
Black, widdow b	12 ,,
Dickson, Thomas, a youth b	14 ,,
Robinson, Bridgit, widdow b	24 ,,

* Entered as Parish Clerk July 18th, 1694—see p. 69 of First Register Book. For John Harding's successor, viz., Richard Page, see p. 57 of this Second Register Book.

Minting, Edward, laborer *b*   24 Mar.

CHRISTENINGS, 1667.

Drewary, William, *s* John and Theodora Drewary *c*   26 ,,
Laines, Sara, *d* William and Sara Laines *c*   10 April
Gouldsborow, Easter, *d* William and Elizabeth Gouldsborow *c*   14 ,,
Looking, Gilbert, *s* Gilbert and Bridgit Looking *c*   28 ,,
Littlebury, Elizabeth, *d* Thomas and Grace Littlebury *c*   7 May
Cockborne, Prissilla, *d* George and Elizabeth Cockborne *c*   6 June
Newman, Henry, *s* John and Penelope Newman *c*   9 ,,
Forman, William, *s* Andrew and Ann Forman *c*   13 ,,
Cooke, Mary, *d* Richard and Margery Cooke *c*   19 ,,
Pell, Robert, *s* Robert and Margaret Pell *c*   29 ,,
Houwood, Robert, *s* Danyell and Ann Houwood *c*   4 Aug.
Markby, Ann, *d* William and Ann Markby *c*   15 ,,
Wigelsworth, George, *s* Edward and Susanna Wigelsworth *c*   18 ,,
Shotten, Elizabeth, *d* Thomas and Susanna Shotten *c*   25 ,,
Westerby, Thomas, *s* Willyam and Sara Westerby *c*   3 Sept.
Bronton, William, *s* John and Ann Bronton *c*   22 ,,
Perkins, Mary, *d* Thomas and Alice Perkins *c*   6 Oct.
Parker, Mary, *d* William and Mary Parker *c*   6 ,,

[Fol. 47*b*.]

Eldred, John, *s* John and Lidia Eldred *c*   27 ,,
Peares, Richard, *s* Ezekiel and Mary Peares *c*   27 ,,
Gooss, Mary, *d* Nathaniel and Bridget Gooss *c*   27 ,,
Martindaile, Judith, *d* Thomas and Judith Martindaile *c*   27 ,,
Stevenson, Mary, *d* Robert and Elizabeth Stevenson *c*   10 Nov.
Minting, Edward, *s* Richard and Elizabeth Minting *c*   17 ,,
Lathorop, Mary, *d* William and Grace Lathorop *c*   19 ,,
Tayler, John, *s* William and Ann Tayler, felmonger *c*   24 ,,
Atkinson, Frances, *d* Edward and Elizabeth Atkinson *c*   1 Dec.
Hamerton, Susanna, *d* Samuell and Susanna Hamerton *c*   8 ,,
Blow, Richard, *s* William and Ann Blow *c*   11 ,,
Wright, Joshua, *s* George and Elizabeth Wright *c*   16 ,,
Bird, Ann, *d* John and Ann Bird *c*   5 Jan.
Tayler, Ann, *d* Robert and Elin Tayler *c*   12 ,,
Chester, Frances, *d* Willyam and Mary Chester *c*   12 ,,
Stubbs, Elizabeth, *d* Thomas and Margaret Stubbs *c*   25 ,,
Bonner, Elizabeth, *d* William and Elizabeth Bonner *c*   2 Feb.
Tayler, Richard, *s* William and Ann Tayler, tanner *c*   13 ,,
Gibson, Sarah, *d* Joseph and Susanna Gibson *c*   16 ,,

[NOTE]—Rich: Page* entered Parish Clark of Horncastle in ye yeare of our Lord God 1666, December the 7.

[Fol. 48*a*.]

Bankes, Bridgit, *d* John and Elizabeth Bankes *c*   18 Feb.
Tarrold, Alice, *d* Paul and Alice Tarrold *c*   8 Mar.
Tunstall, Elizabeth, *d* Edmund and Milldred Tunstall *c*   8 ,,
Richinson, Margerie, *d* John and Helen Richinson *c*   19 ,,
Burton, Mary, *d* Thomas and Ann Burton *c*   22 ,,

MARRIAGES, 1667.

Tayler, Frances }
Cooke, Mary   } *m*   30 April

Dauson, Edward }
West, Mary   } *m*   30 ,,

Poule, John }
Gillam, Ann } *m*   1 May

Clarke, William }
Johnson, Martha } *m*   7 ,,

* See p. 56 for burial of John Harding, Rich. Page's predecessor.

Rouoth, Edward Beverley, Judith } m		9 May
Poule, Edward Moltby, Mary } m		4 June
Richlson, John Bucknall, Ellin } m		13 ,,
Tharrold, John Smith, Dorothie } m		18 ,,
Beverley, Mr. George Gibson, Mrs. Anna } m		4 July
Dixon, William Smith, Ann } m		17 Sept.
Wigelsworth, Edward Goode, Elizabeth } m		23 ,,
Graves, William Wright, Margaret } m		24 ,.
Cocker, Henery Couper, Elizabeth } m		24 ,,
Gibson, Roger Forman, Mary } m		26 Nov
Clarke, Micaiell Thompson, Ann } m		5 Sept
Wells, Thomas Shelley, Alice } m		19 Dec.
Barron, William Barnard, Martha } m		14 Jan.
Marshall, Thomas Goulsborow, Margaret } m		30 ,,
Sallmon, Edward Knight, Ann } m		4 Feb.

BURIALLS, 1667.

Moyser, John, a youth b		29 Mar.
Snoden, Scroub, gent. b		30 ,,
Briggs, Ann, widdow b		6 April
Claith, Richard b		28 ,,
Curtis, Robert b		2 May
Littlebury, Elizabeth, an infant b		15 ,,
Eldred, Lidia, an infant b		19 ,,
Gill, John, labourer b		25 ,,
Cooke, Mary, an infant b		26 ,,
Beverly, Ciscily, wife John Beverley b		31 July
Parker, Edward, a tayler b		6 Aug.
Brian, Robert a scrivener, uor [or] curate b		7 ,,
Broune, Thomas, an infant b		10 ,,
Tayler, Joseph, a youth b		15 ,,
Dixon, Charles, an infant b		17 ,,
Pasmore, William, sadler b		17 ,,
Toffe, Mary, spinster b		17 ,,

[Fol. 48b]

Cooke, Ann, widdow b		18 ,,
Wigelsworth, Susanna, wife Edward Wigelsworth b		19 ,,
Westland, Mary, spinster b		26 ,,
Wright, Margaret, widdow b		30 ,,
Wells, Elizabeth, widdow b		31 ,,
Eldin, Ann, an infant b		2 Sept.
Mason, Elizabeth, wife Nicholas Mason		3 ,,
Westeby, Thomas b		4 ,,
Chester, Frances, an infant b		15 ,,
Dixon, Thomas, an infant b		20 ,,

Abe, James, a joyner *b* — 2 Oct.
Wigellsworth, Ann, wife Edmund Wigellsworth *b* — 3 ,,
Sallmon, Ester, widdow *b* — 20 ,,
Wigellsworth, George, an infant *b* — 26 ,,
Locking, Gilbert, an infant *b* — 30 ,,
Wells, Mary, wife Thomas Wells, felmonger *b* — 4 Nov.
Leach, Sarah, wife Richard Leach, draper *b* — 18 ,,
Wright, Margaret, wife John Wright *b* — 19 ,,
Goulsborow, Briggit, widdow *b* — 22 ,,
Martindale, Judith, an infant *b* — 22 ,,
Minting, Edward, an infant *b* — 28 ,,
Johnson, Richard *b* — 5 Dec.
Walsher, Elizabeth, widdow *b* — 8 ,,
Wright, Jossua, an infant *b* — 19 ,,
Marr, Amey, an infant *b* — 22 ,,
Wigelsworth, Edmund *b* — 25 ,,
Clarke, Francis *b* — 31 ,,
Marshall, Jone, wife Thomas Marshall *b* — 8 Jan.
Bird, Ann, an infant *b* — 9 ,,
Bautery, William, an apothecary *b* — 11 ,,
Huddleston, Briggit, an infant *b* — 13 ,,
Hamerton, Thomas, felmonger *b* — 16 ,,
Gibson, Susanna, wife William Gibson *b* — 6 Feb.
Longley, Sarah *b* — 12 ,,
Laines, William, a youth *b* — 15 ,,
Bankes, Briggit, an infant *b* — 19 ,,
Stevenson, Robert, laborour *b* — 28 ,,
Skinney, William *b* — 28 ,,
Martindalle, Judith, an infant *b* — 1 Mar.
Bulivant, Mary, spinster *b* — 7 ,,
Wright, Alice, wife Thomas Wright *b* — 8 ,,
Shotton, Edward *b* — 9 ,,
Richlson, Margery, an infant *b* — 20 ,,

[Fol. 49a.]

CHRISTENINGS, 1668.

Beverley, Elizabeth, *d.* M*r* George Beverley and Anna his wife *c* — 30 Mar.
Marley, Henery, *s.* Jonathan and Ann Marley *c* — 1 April
Marr, John, *s.* Robert and Elizabeth Marr *c* — 5 ,,
Tinker, Thomas, *s.* Thomas and Ann Tinker *c* — 5 ,,
Clapam, Robet, *s.* Raalph and May Clapam *c* — 5 ,,
Clarke, Mildred, *d.* William and Martha Clarke, Glasman *c* — 12 ,,
Hancock, John, *s.* John and Alice Hancock *c* — 26 ,,
Chamberlaine, John, *s.* John and Joan Chamberlaine *c* — 28 ,,
Garnnis, Susan, *d.* James and Mary Garnnis *c* — 17 May
Browne, Thomas, *s.* Jeremiah and Isabell Browne, whitesmith *c* — 24 ,,
Tharrold, Jane, *d.* John and Dorothy Tharrold *c* — 19 ,,
Gentle, Ann, *d.* Benjamin and Elizabeth Gentle *c* — 2 Aug.
Brockey, William, the bastard child of Martha Brockey, and
    putative of William Bautery *c* — 5 ,,
Gibon, Thomas, *s.* John and Elizabeth Gibon *c* — 23 ,,
Houlderness, Thomas, *s.* John and Frances Houlderness *c* — 30 ,,
Kerk, Sarah, *d.* William and Mary Kerk *c* — 6 Sept.
Litlebury, John, *s.* Thomas and Grace Litlebury, draper *c* — 10 ,,
Gibson, George, *s.* Roger and Mary Gibson *c* — 15 ,,
Harkoom, Ann, *d.* John and Lidia Harkoom *c* — 27 ,,
Smith, Mary, *d.* Thomas and Elizabeth Smith, mason *c* — 27 ,,
Wilson, Elizabeth, *d.* Gilbert and Mary Wilson *c* — 4 Oct.

Locking, Mary, *d.* Gilbert and Bridgit Locking *c*   9 Oct.
Dixson, Ann, *d.* William and Ann Dixson *b*   18 ,,

[Fol. 49*b*.]

Martindaile, John, *s.* Thomas and Judith Martindaile *c*   25 ,,
Graves, Ann, *d.* William and Margery Blades *c*   26 Nov.
Ostlin, Thomas, *s.* Thomas and Mary Ostlin *c*   30 ,,
Houdlestone, Trustrum, *s* Hamlet and Margaret Houdlestone *c*   13 Dec.
Markby, Ann, *d.* Hastens and Ann Markby *c*   2 Jan.
Dauson, Peter, *s.* Thomas and Magdalen Dauson *c*   3 ,,
Crosby, Roger, *s.* Richard and Ann Crossby *c*   6 ,,
Wigelsworth, Elizabeth, *d.* Edward and Elizabeth Wigelsworth *c* 6 ,,
Martindaile, Ann, *d.* Robert and Mary Martindaile *c*   10 ,,
Cater, Elizabeth, *d.* Richard and Mary Cater *c*   19 ,,
Haward, Ann, *d.* Daniell and Ann Haward *c*   24 ,,
Westerby, Bridgit, *d.* William and Sarah Westerby *c*   31 ,,
Tuxworth, George, *s.* Steaven and Mary Tuxworth *c*   14 Feb.
Francis, Wiat, *s.* Hermon and Elizabeth Francis *c*   23 ,,
Jacson, Hester, *d.* John Jacson, strainger *c*   29 ,,
Dailes, Joab, *s.* John and Hellen Dailes *c*   14 Mar.
Ascough, John, *s.* Francis and Margaret Ascough *c*   23 ,,

MARRIAGES, 1668.

Middleton, Thomas ⎱ *m* with a licence   21 May
Young, Susanna ⎰

Woollmore, Cromwell ⎱ *m*   18 Jan.
Browne, Elizabeth ⎰

Parker, Charles ⎱ *m*   22 ,,
Bauderick, Bridget ⎰

Enderby, John ⎱ *m*   30 July
Grismon, Mary ⎰

Macaris, John ⎱ *m* with a licence   10 Aug.
Stob, Elizabeth ⎰

Goake, John ⎱ *m*   18 ,,
Walles, Elizabeth ⎰

Gibson, Thomas ⎱ *m*   20 ,,
Johnson, Elizabeth ⎰

Wright, Thomas ⎱ *m*   29 Sept.
Abe, Mary ⎰

Hollingshead, Lawrence ⎱ *m*   1 Oct.
Johnson, Elizabeth ⎰

Groves, George ⎱ *m*   1 ,,
Bilitin, Martha ⎰

[Fol. 50*a*.]

Mason, Nicholas ⎱ *m*   27 ,,
Hudlestone, Isabell ⎰

Lease, William ⎱ *m*   26 Nov.
Shotten, Ellen ⎰

Husey, John ⎱ *m*   6 Jan.
Latherop, Susanna ⎰

Hinde, Thomas ⎱ *m*   23 Feb.
Thomson, Elizabeth ⎰

BURIALLS, 1668.

Richeson, Ellen, wife John Richeson *b*   28 Mar.
Beverley, Elizabeth, an infant *b*   31 ,,
Richeson, Richard, adolescence *b*   7 April
Bruton, Richard, adolesence *b*   17 ,,

Curtis, Margery, widow *b*	22 April
Rouksby, Elizabeth, virginis *b*	6 May
Garnes, Susanna, an infant *b*	17 ,,
Richoson, Thomas, taylor *b*	1 June
Tinker, Thomas, an infant *b*	1 ,,
Newman, William, an infant *b*	15 ,,
Howard, Robert, an infant *b*	26 ,,
Forman, Edward, blacksmith *b*	16 July
Wells, Henry, ar a paritte (*sic*) *b*	19 ,,
Skellton, Elizabeth, widow *b*	3 Aug.
Boulton, Mary, widow *b*	19 ,,
Parish, Ellen, wife John Parish *b*	20 ,,
Sallmon, Ann, wife of Edward Sallmon *b*	1 Sept.
Page, John, an infant *b*	2 Oct.
Waters, Richard, of Edlington *b*	5 ,,
Vry, Alice, widow *b*	10 ,,
Looking, Mary, an infant *b*	11 ,,
Dixon, Ann, wife William Dixon *b*	18 ,,
Endeby, Susanna, wife William Endeby *b*	19 ,,
Falles, John, laborer *b*	21 ,,
Tharrold, Alice, an infant *b*	21 ,,
Hindes, Frances, wife Thomas Hindes *b*	30 ,,
Gibson, Thomas, an infant *b*	31 ,,
Atkinson, Frances, an infant *b*	28 Nov.
Nellsie, Protacia, widow *b*	12 Dec.
Huddlestone, Trestrum, an infant *b*	18 ,,
Huddlestone, Mary, an infant *b*	21 ,,
Tysdall, Mary, wife Robert Tysdall *b*	1 Jan.
Markby, Ann, an infant *b*	3 ,,
Kerk, Sarah, an infant *b*	5 ,,
Butler, Samuell, a youth *b*	7 ,,
Crosby, Roger, an infant *b*	7 ,,
Wigelsworth, Elizabeth, an infant *b*	9 ,,
Parker, Bridget, wife Charles Parker *b*	29 ,,
Pouderill, Richard, Junior *b*	28 ,,
Littlebury, William *b*	2 Feb.

[Fol. 50b.]

Bauderick, Margery, widow of Maram *b*	3 ,,
Skipley, John, of South Willingham *b*	19 ,,
James, Ann, wife Thomas James, draper *b*	22 ,,
Francis, Wiat, an infant *b*	2 Mar.
Leake, Richard *b*	9 ,,
Burton, Mary, an infant *b*	9 ,,
Littlebury, John, an infant *b*	10 ,,

Here endeth Burialls.

CHRISTENINGS, 1669.

Towitt, Ann, *d.* Edward and Elizabeth Towitt *c*	28 Mar.
Cocker, Henry, *s.* Henry and Elizabeth Cocker *c*	2 April
Goude, Joseph, *s.* Thomas and Mary Goude *c*	7 ,,
Gibon, Thomas, *s.* Thomas and —— Gibon *c*	11 ,,
Minting, Ann, *d.* Richard and Elizabeth Minting *c*	11 ,,
Drury, Charles, *s.* John and Thudery Drury *c*	14 ,,
West, Richard, *s.* Nathaniel and Elizabeth West *c*	25 ,,
Lawrence, Robert, *s.* Hollingshead and Elizabeth Lawrence *c*	9 May
Tayler, John, *s.* Robert and Ellen Tayler, glover *c*	23 ,,
Tayler, Elizabeth. *d.* William and Ann Tayler, fellmonger *c*	23 ,,
Gibson, Ann, *d.* Thomas and Elizabeth Gibson, butcher *c*	23 ,,

Haines, Charles, *s.* Charles and Ellen Haines *c*	1 June
Gillam, Elizabeth, *d.* Thomas and Elizabeth Gillam *c*	20 ,,
Bird, John, *s.* John and Ann Bird, tanner *c*	25 ,,
Dove, Susanna, *d.* Mr. Samuell and Katherine Dove *c*	6 July
Maccaris, Barbara, *d.* John and Elizabeth Maccaris, tanner *c*	11 ,,
Fouller, Thomas, *s.* Robert and Mary Fouller *c*	18 ,,
Lathrop, William, *s.* William and Grace Lathrop *c*	80 ,,

[Fol. 51a.]

Thorold, Paul, *s.* Paul and Alice Thorold *c*	5 Sept.
Goakes, Ann, *d.* John and Elizabeth Goakes *c*	5 ,,
Broughton, Ann, *d.* John and Ann Broughton *c*	12 ,,
Chester, William, *s.* William and Mary Chester *c*	26 ,,
Cockborne, Mary, *d.* George and Elizabeth Cockborne *c*	31 ,,
Cooke, Richard, *s.* Richard and Margery Cooke *c*	9 Oct.
Dawson, Mary, *d.* Edward and Mary Dawson *c*	14 ,,
Garnes, Richard, *s.* James and Mary Garnes *c*	17 ,,
Markby, Jane, *d.* William and Ann Markby *c*	2 Nov.
Tayler, Grace, *d.* Francis and Mary Tayler yᵉ younger *c*	28 ,,
Locking, John, *s.* Gilbert and Bridget Locking *c*	28 ,,
Gibson, Thomas, *s.* Roger and Mary Gibson *c*	28 ,,
Knight, Ann, *d.* Robert and Mary Knight *c*	28 ,,
Newman, John, *s.* John and Penellope Newman *c*	19 Dec.
Shepard, Mary, *d.* Walter and Lucie Shepard *c*	23 ,,
West, Steven, *s.* John and Ann West *c*	26 ,,
Simson, William, *s.* John and Elizabeth Simson *c*	26 ,,
Husey, John, *s.* John and Susanna Husey *c*	30 ,,
Shotten, Ann, *d.* Thomas and Susanna Shotten *c*	2 Jan.
Markby, Ann, *d.* Hastens and Ann Markby *c*	16 ,,
Burton, John, *s.* Thomas and Ann Burton *c*	22 ,,
Kerk, William, *s.* Richard and Ann Kerk *c*	28 ,,

[Fol. 51b.]

Grove, Jane, *d.* Augustine and Jane Grove *c*	28 ,,
Tunstall, Jonathan, *s.* Edmund and Mildred Tunstall *c*	27 ,,
Marley, Joshua, *s.* Joshua and Mary Marley *c*	30 ,,
Marr, William, *s.* Robert and Elizabeth Marr *c*	13 Feb.
Haward, John, *s,* Dainyell and Ann Haward *c*	20 Mar.
Gibson, Elizabeth, *d.* Joseph and Susanna Gibson *c*	20 ,,

Here endeth Christenings, 1669.

MARRIAGES, 1669.

Tysdall, Robert Lowson, Margaret	*m*	6 May
Richardson, John Curtis, Anne	*m*	6 ,,
Bellammie, Richard Barron, Elizabeth	*m*	6 ,,
Endeby, William Frankiss, Isabell	*m*	11 ,,
Dennis, Richard Tunstall, Jane	*m*	13 ,,
Croskill, Richard Leake, Prissilla	*m*	9 Nov.
Woodthorpe, John Stubbs, Elizabeth	*m*	13 Jan.

Bonner, John }
Flinton, Ann } *m*   13 Jan.

Holbitch, Richard }
Summerscales, Ann } *m*   31 „

BURIALS, 1669.

Kerk, Francis, an infant *b*   29 Mar.
Willyamson, Elizabeth, wife John Willyamson *b*   9 April
Francis, Thomas, an infant *b*   26 „
Brockby, William, the bastard child of Martha Brockby *b*   2 May
Brotherton, Elizabeth, an infant *b*   8 „
Marley, Henry, an infant *b*   3 „
Wells, Susanna, Virginis *b*   17 „
West, Richard, an infant *b*   28 „
Ascough, John, an infant *b*   28 „
Tailer, Ann, an infant *b*   29 „
Shepard, Katherine, the wife of Waters Shepard *b*   4 June
Martindale, Ann, wife Christopher Martindale *b*   6 „
Tailer, John, an infant *b*   25 „
Bonner, Elizabeth, an infant *b*   5 July
Redthorne, Elizebeth, wife Thomas Redthorne *b*   5 Aug.
Macoris, Barbara, an infant *b*   10 „
Carr, Thomas, shoemaker *b*   27 „
Grason, Edward, laborer *b*   29 „

[Fol. 52a.]

Gibson, Mary, *d.* Mr. Thomas Gibson, Vicar of Horncastle *b*   30 „
Leafe, William *b*   1 Sept.
Goake, Ann, an infant *b*   17 „
Denvers, Eusaby *b*   19 „
Cheesbrook, Elizabeth, widow *b*   20 „
Endeby, Margaret, wife Thomas Endeby *b*   26 „
Groves, John, an infant *b*   11 Oct.
Cooke, Richard, an infant *b*   19 „
Poule, Efraim, a youth *b*   9 Nov.
Broadley, Richard, Muisition *b*   12 „
Johnson, Thomas, a youth *b*   2 Dec.
Tailor, Grace, an infant *b*   2 „
Hamerton, Margaret, widow *b*   15 „
Parish, John, Tailor *b*   19 „
Wright, John, bucher *b*   4 Jan.
Simpson, William, an infant *b*   10 „
Wells, Thomas, felmonger *b*   15 „
Wells, Thomas, Junior, fellmonger *b*   20 „
Clarke, Martha, wife William Clarke *b*   25 „
Toyn, Robert, of Darwood *b*   27 Feb.
Thulis, Bridgit, widow *b*   27 „
Laurence, Robert, an infant *b*   28 „
Smith, Ann, wife Mr. Steven Smith *b*   1 Mar.
West, Nathanyell *b*   4 „
Hamerton, Thomas, Tanner *b*   6 „
Freeston, Alice, widow *b*   11 „

CHRISTENINGS.

Artera, Mary, *d.* John and Mary Artera *c*   27 „
Littlebury, John, *s.* Thomas and Grace Littlebury *c*   29 „
Richardson, Mary, *d.* John and Ann Richardson *c*   10 April
Skill, Mary, *d.* William and Ellen Skill *c*   10 „

- Coling, Jaine, *d.* Thomas and Alice Coling *c*   14 April
- Hamnett, Elizabeth, *d.* John and Ann Hamnett *c*   26 „

[Fol. 52*b*.]

- Dixon, John, *s.* John and Elizabeth Dixon, carrier *c*   8 May
- Graves, Liddia, *d.* William and Margery Graves *c*   20 „
- Cocker, Amey, *d.* Henry and Elizabeth Cocker *c*   7 June
- Francis, Thomas, *s.* John and Mary Francis, felmonger *c*   3 July
- Freston, Robert, *s.* Thomas and Grace Freston, gent *c*   12 „
- Bennett, Elizabeth, *d.* Martin and Sarah Bennett, ironmonger *c* 13 „
- Markby, Jonathan, *s.* Jonathan and Ann Markby *c*   21 „
- Marshall, Richard, *s.* Thomas and Margaret Marshall *c*   8 Aug.
- Kerk, William, *s.* William and Mary Kerk *c*   29 „
- Maccaris, Mary, *d.* John and Elizabeth Maccaris *c*   11 Sep.
- Nayler, Susanna, *d.* Robert and Elvin Nayler *c*   14 „
- Goake, John, *s.* John and Elizabeth Goake, felmonger *c*   16 „
- Hamerton, Thomas, *s.* Samuel and Susanna Hamerton *c* 21 „
- Wigellsworth, Ann, *d.* Edward and Elizabeth Wigellsworth *c* 2 Oct.
- Tayler, Ann, *d.* William and Ann Tayler, felmonger *c*   16 „
- Cooke, William, *s.* Richard and Margery Cooke *c*   22 „
- Ascough, Thomas, *s.* Francis and Margaret Ascough *c*   10 Nov.
- Tharrold, James, *s.* John and Dorothy Tharrold *c*   17 „
- Gibon, William, *s.* John and Elizabeth Gibon *c*   27 „
- Kerk, Katherine, *d.* Richard and Ann Kerk *c*   23 Dec.
- Houltby, Anne, *d.* Richard and Ann Houltby *c*   29 „

[Fol. 53*a*.]

Hancock, Nicholas, *s.* John and Alice Hancock *c*   8 Jan.
- Bichfield, Elizabeth, *d.* John and Ann Bichfield *c*   15 „
- Browne, John, *s.* Jeremiah and Isabell Browne *c*   15 „
Hollinghead, Joseph, *s.* Joseph and Elizabeth Hollinghead, 17 „
    labreure *c*
- Enderby, Robert, *s.* Thomas and Ann Enderby, tayler *c*   18 „
- Hamerton, Edmund, *s.* John and Ruth Hamerton, tanner *c* 26 „
- Peares, John, *s.* Ezekiale and Mary Peares *c*   5 Feb.
- Dennis, Robert, *s.* Richard and Jaine Dennis *c*   28 „
- Hanley, Ann, *d.* John and Isabele Hanley *c*   5 Mar.
- Blow, John, *s.* William and Ann Blow *c*   19 „

Here endeth Christenings.

MARRIAGES, 1670

- Willingson, John
- Kellsay, Debora } *m*   12 April
- Hamerton, John
- Pinshbeck, Ruth } *m*   12 „
- Boulton, George
- Clarke, Ann } *m*   12 „
- Tayler, Thomas
- Craftes, Ann } *m*   8 May
- Westland, Richard
- Broughton, Elizabeth } *m*   8 „
- Enderby, Thomas
- Gibson, Ann } *m*   30 „
- Tayler, William
- Houkrom, Elizabeth } *m*   18 June
- Curtis, John
- Bradley, Ann } *m*   19 July
Hauley, John
- Gresham, Isabele } *m*   10 Sep.
- Goosse, Nathaniele
- Peake, Margaret } *m*   19 „

Parker, Charles Baines, Elizabeth } *m*		29 Sep,
Dudick, Thomas Nicholes, Bridgit } *m*		29 ,,
Hamerton, Thomas Hareby, Ann } *m*		11 Oct.
Marley, Jonathan Cater, Elizabeth } *m*		20 ,,
Bowring, James Stevenson, Elizabeth } *m*		27 ,,
Maddison, Christopher Hamerton, Elizabeth } *m*		4 Dec.
Deane, John Porson, Mary } *m*		15 ,,
Toyney, Peter Maver, Mary } *m*		3 Jan.
Richardson, John, Drury, Elizabeth } *m*		17 ,,
Looking, John Williamson, Mary } *m*		9 Mar.
Loverick, Mathew Carr, Mary } *m*		23 ,,

[Fol. 53*b*.]

BURIALLS, 1670.

Burton, John, adolesence *b*	15 April
Smiton, John, of Marem in ye Fern *b*	20 ,,
Richardson, Ann, wife John Richardson *b*	27 ,,
Richardson, Mary, an infant *b*	7 May
Fouler, Georges, an infant *b*	26 ,,
Clarke, Joane, wife Richard Clarke *b*	28 ,,
Gathsle, John, a youth *b*	7 June
Browned Elizabeth, widow *b*	21 ,,
Goosse, Bridgit, wife Nathaniell Goosse *b*	13 July
Williman, Mary virginis *b*	20 ,,
Marley, Ann, wife Jonathan Marley *b*	31 ,,
Brouton, Ann, wife John Brouton *b*	8 Aug.
Marshall, Richard, an infant *b*	20 ,,
Shotten, Ann, an infant *b*	27 ,,
Francis, Thomas, an infant *b*	27 ,,
Clapam, Elizabeth, widow *b*	18 ,,
Goake, John, an infant *b*	27 ,,
Johnson, Ester, widow *b*	19 Sep.
Bocock, Lucie, spinster *b*	28 ,,
Wigelsworth, Ann, an infant *b*	9 Oct.
Castledoune, Ester, widow *b*	18 ,,
Gibson, William, translator *b*	8 Nov.
Gibon, William, an infant *b*	3 Dec.
Parker, Robert, balife *b*	5 ,,
Locking, Ellen, wife John Locking *b*	14 ,,
Nightcalles, William, tanner *b*	17 ,,
Bonner, Alan, adolesence *b*	21 ,,
Newman, William, an infant *b*	7 Jan.
Hawkins, Elizabeth, wife George Hawkins *b*	14 ,,
Browne, Thomas, laborer *b*	17 ,,
Tayler, Elizabeth, an infant *b*	21 ,,
Willingson, John, laborer *b*	24 ,,
Craftes, Henry, cutler *b*	12 Feb.
Browne, Elizabeth, an infant *b*	15 ,,

Gibson, Joseph, couper *b*	16	Feb.
Houldrige, Ann, an infant *b*	20	,,
Wright, George, an infant *b*	24	,,
Peares, Mary, wife Ezekiele Peares *b*	1	Mar.
Dinnis, Robert, an infant *b*	8	,,
Puge, Thomas, adolesence *b*	12	,,
Bonner, Elizabeth, widow *b*	12	,,
Croskill, Prissilla, wife Richard Croskill *b*	15	,,
Houlden, Thomas, an infant *b*	22	,,
Endeble, William, laborer *b*	28	,,

[Fol. 54a.]

CHRISTENINGS, 1671.

Adison, Joseph, *s.* Charles and Mary Adison *c*	26	,,
Harkconne, Mary, *d.* John and Lidia Harkconne *c*	8	April
Minting, Richard, *s.* Richard and Elizabeth Minting *c*	9	,,
Dawson, David, *s.* Thomas and Magdelen Dawson *c*	9	,,
Husey, Sarah, *d.* John and Susanna Husey *c*	19	,,
Ranby, John, *s.* John and Mary Ranby *c*	23	,,
Howgrave, Elizabeth, *d.* Alexander and Elizabeth Howgrave *c*	2	May
Thorrald, John, *s.* Paul and Alice Thorrald *c*	3	,,
Haines, Ann, *d.* Charles and Ellen Haines *c*	6	,,
Tunstall, Edmund, *s.* Edmund and Mildred Tunstall *c*	30	,,
Chearles, Elianor, *d.* Mr. Richard and Elizabeth Chearles *c*	6	June
Grimson, Nazereth, *d.* John and Elizabeth Grimson *c*	11	,,
Page, Nicholas, *s.* Thomas and Frances Page *c*	14	,,
Chester, John, *s* William and Mary Chester *c*	18	,,
Curtis, Thomas, *s.* John and Ann Curtis *c*	18	,,
Clapam, Elizabeth, *d.* Ralph and Mary Clapam *c*	25	,,
Dailes, Lidia, *d.* John and Hester Dailes *c*	9	July
Freston, Thomas, *s.* Mr. Thomas and Grace Freston, gent *c*	10	,,
Cockborne, George, *s.* George and Elizabeth Cockborne, mercer *c*	4	Aug.

[Fol. 54b.]

Skill, Elizabeth, *d.* William and Ellen Skill *c*	16	,,
Scaman, Faith, *d.* Edward and Mary Scaman *c*	25	,,
Eldred, William, *s.* John and Lidia Eldred *c*	27	,,
Parker, Elizabeth, *d.* Charles and Elizabeth Parker *c*	5	Sep.
Tayler, John, *s.* Francis and Mary Tayler *c*	17	,,
Broughton, Richard, *s.* Robert and —— Broughton *c*	5	Oct.
Marshall, Ann, *d.* Thomas and Margaret Marshall *c*	27	,,
Poule, John, *s.* Edward and Mary Poule *c*	9	Nov.
Shoton, Edward, *s.* Thomas and Susanna Shoton *c*	12	,,
Touill, Elizabeth, *d* Edward and Elizabeth Touill *c*	12	,,
Houldeness, Jeremiah, *s.* John and Frances Houldeness *c*	19	,,
Lathrop, Elizabeth, *d.* William and Grace Lathrop *c*	23	,,
Bird, Miles, *s.* John and Ann Bird, tanner *c*	24	,,
Wells, Thomas, *s.* Thomas and Alice Wells, tanner *c*	14	Dec.
Morgan, Jane, *d.* Robert and Jane Morgan, a stranger *c*	17	,,
Markby, Hustens, *s.* Hustens and Ann Markby *c*	18	,,
Bowling, Elizabeth, *d.* James and Elizabeth Bowing *c*	30	,,
Cocker, Thomas, *s.* Henry and Elizabeth Cocker *c*	12	Jan.
Tayler, Faith, *d.* Robert and Ellen Tayler, glover *c*	14	,,
Locking, Mary, *d.* Gilbert and Bridgit Locking *c*	21	,,
Maddison, Christofer, *s.* Christofer and Elizabeth Maddison *c*	30	,,
Swindall, Elizabeth, *d.* Robert and Catherine Swindall *c*	11	Feb.

[Fol. 55a.]

Goake, John, *s.* John and Elizabeth Goake *c*	15	,,
Wigellsworth, Edward, *s.* Edward and Elizabeth Wigellsworth carrier *c*	1	Mar.

— Dixon, William, *s*. John and Elizabeth Dixon, Carrier *c* .... 1 Mar.
—Francis, Elizabeth, *d*. John and Mary Francis *c* .... 10 ,,
- Butler, Frances, *d*. Joseph and Elizabeth Butler *c* .... 12 ,,
- Husey, Thomas, *s*. John and Susanna Husey, mercer *c* .... 14 ,,
- Husey, Charles, *s*. John and Susanna Husey, mercer *c* .... 19 ,,
—Forman, Ann, *d*. Andrew and Ann Forman *c* .... 24 ,,
- Gibon, Thomas, *s*. Thomas and Jane Gibon *c* .... 24 ,,
- Kerk, Debora, *d*. Richard and Ann Kerk *c* .... 24 ,,
—Garnes, Priscilla, *d*. James and Mary Garnes *c* .... 24 ,,

Here endeth Christenings.

MARRIAGES, 1671.

—Swindall, Robert } *m* .... 4 May
- Gray, Catherin }

—Bonner, William } *m* .... 9 ,,
—Tayler, Martha }

—Gibon, Thomas } *m* .... 22 June
—Houlton, Jane }

—Newman, John } *m* .... 3 Aug.
—Charter, Ann }

- Bumris, William } *m* .... 5 ,,
- Pouderill, Ann }

- Bradley, John } *m* .... 17 ,,
—Webster, Mary }

- Clarke, Anthony } *m* .... 12 Sept.
—Lease, Ellen }

- Eyre, Thomas } *m* .... 28 Nov.
—Bust, Elizabeth }

—Martindayle, Robert } *m* .... 28 ,,
—Cousin, Sarah }

Addison, Thomas } *m* .... 30 ,,
—Carter, Mary }

- James, Thomas } *m* .... 5 Dec.
- Pinder, Elizabeth }

Birch, Thomas } *m* .... 24 ,,
—How, Faith }

—Frith, William } *m* .... 25 ,,
—Clarke, Mary }

—Benton, John } *m* .... 13 Feb.
- Wright, Elizabeth }

[Fol. 55b.]

BURIALLS, 1671.

- Powderill, Richard *b* .... 26 Mar.
- Adison, Joseph *b* .... 28 ,,
—Law, Esther, widow *b* .... 31 ,,
- Martindaile, Mary, wife Robert Martindaile *b* .... 5 April
- Greaves, Richard, an infant *b* .... 6 ,,
- Francis, Mary, wife Thomas Francis *b* .... 8 ,,
—Burton, M^{rs}. widow *b* .... 8 ,,
- Hanson, Francis *b* .... 11 ,,
—Harcome, Mary, an infant *b* .... 12 ,,
—Gibson, Elizabeth, an infant *b* .... 24 ,,
- Stubbs, Peter, glazier *b* .... 27 ,,
—Stavers, Gydo, shomaker *b* .... 27 ,,
- Tharold, Thomas, malster *b* .... 28 ,,
—Smith, Mary, widow *b* .... 28 ,,
—Bichfield, Margaret, widow *b* .... 2 May
—Walker, Margery, spinster *b* .... 4 ,,

- Tharold, John, an infant *b*	21	May
- Newman, Penelope, wife John Newman *b*	7	June
- Browne, Elizabeth, a traveller *b*	16	,,
- Douse, Margaret, an infant *b*	22	,,
- Mayrs, Elizabeth, spinster *b*	28	,,
- Curtis, Thomas, an infant *b*	28	,,
- Husey, Sarah, an infant *b*	7	July
- Eyre, Bridgit. wife Thomas Eyre *b*	81	,,
- Ascough, Thomas, an infant *b*	1	Aug.
- Tayler, Christopher, a youth *b*	7	,,
- Howgrave, Elizabeth, an infant *b*	9	,,
- Cockburn, George, an infant *b*	10	,,
- Peares, Richard, an infant *b*	20	,,
- Martindale, John, an infant *b*	24	,,
- Scamon, Faith, an infant *b*	27	,,
- Clarke, Catherine, spinster *b*	28	,,
- Adison, Mary, an infant *b*	29	,,
- Parker, Elizabeth, an infant *b*	4	Sept.
- Scamon, ——, wife Edward Scamon *b*	14	,,
- Westband, William. a youth *b*	19	,,
- Loverick, Thomas, a youth *b*	22	,,
- Lawson, Mary, a widow *b*	25	,,
- Haines, John, an infant *b*	2	Oct.
- Fitch, Nathanial, adolescence *b*	2	,,
- Broughton. Richard, an infant *b*	6	,,
- Hancock, Stephen, an infant *b*	12	,,
- Fowler, Mary, an infant *b*	12	,,
- Derby, Robert, adolescence *b*	18	,,
- Clapam, Elisabeth, an infant *b*	9	Nov.
- Poule, John, an infant *b*	13	,,
- Marr, William, an infant *b*	17	,,
- Barron, William, laborer *b*	18	,,
- Parish, Ann, spinster *b*	21	,,
- Parpoynt, Robert, adolescence *b*	27	,,
- Markby, Ann, spinster *b*	27	,,
- Richardson, Ann, spinster *b*	10	Dec.
- Bird, Miles, an infant *b*	13	,,
- Perkins, Mary, an infant *b*	20	,,
- Smith, Christopher, yeoman *b*	24	,,
- Bowring, James, Cooper *b*	19	Jan.
- Madeus, Edward, Tayler *b*	4	Feb.

[Fol. 56a.]

- Wallshere, Leonard, a youth *b*	22	,,
- Tayler, Faith, an infant *b*	24	,,
- Houldridge, Edmund, courd winder *b*	28	,,
- Wigellsworth, Edward, an infant *b*	3	Mar.
- Marshall, Thomas, Tayler *b*	4	,,
- Haines, Ann, an infant *b*	5	,,
- Gentiche, Ann, an infant *b*	8	,,
- Ranby, Dorothy, Widow *b*	9	,,
- Adison, Charles, Milliner *b*	12	,,
- Beeton, John, adolescence *b*	12	,,
- Tharold, James, an infant *b*	18	,,
- Minting, Ann, an infant *b*	21	,,

CHRISTENINGS, 1672.

- Brobue, Thomas, *s.* George and Mary Brobue *c*	27	Mar.
- Colling, Marth, *d.* Thomas and Ann Colling *c*	31	,,

Nichols, Mary, the bastard child of Anne Nicholls, and putative of John Riggs c	8 April	
Graves, William, s. William and Margery Graves c	9 ,,	
Lamaman, { William, Robert, } ss. Robert & Elizabeth Lamaman c	17 ,,	
Perkins, Susanna, d. Thomas and Alice Perkins c	17 ,,	
Gibon, Vincent, s. Thomas and Esther Gibon c	21 ,,	
Richardson, John, s. John and Elizabeth Richardson c	21 ,,	
Broughton, Mary, d. John and Mary Broughton c	28 ,,	
Meanwell, John, s. John and Ameleis Meanwell c	8 May	
Houltridge, Frances, d. Richard and Ann Houltridge c	13 ,,	
Newman, William, s. John and Ann Newman c	26 ,,	
Grovine, Mary, d. Thomas and Ester Grovine c	26 ,,	
Ranby, Mary, d. John and Mary Ranby c	11 June	
Westeby, Sarah, d. William and Sarah Westeby c	16 ,,	
Perkins, Robert, s. Robert and Mary Perkins c	25 ,,	
Smith, Elizabeth, d. Thomas and Elizabeth Smith, mason c	30 ,,	

[Fol. 56b.]

Gentil, Bridgit, d. Benjamin and Elizabeth Gentil c	7 July	
Douse, Sarah, d. Thomas and Elizabeth Douse c	7 ,,	
Markby, John, s. William and Ann Markby, barber c	18 ,,	
Cooke, Francis, s. Francis and Martha Cooke c	18 ,,	
Tayler, Ann, d. William and Ann Tayler, tanner c	21 ,,	
Maccris, John, s. John and Ellen Macckris, fellmonger c	28 ,,	
Bradley, John, s. John and Mary Bradley c	11 Aug.	
Tayler, Elizabeth, d. William and Ann Tayler, fellmonger c	18 ,,	
Harcome, Jane, d. John and Liddia Harcome c	18 ,,	
Hamerton, Mary, d. Thomas and Ann Hamerton, fellmonger c	25 ,,	
Ascouth, Frances, d. Francis and Margaret Ascouth c	27 ,,	
Frith, William, s. William and Mary Frith, barber c	4 Sept.	
Haward, Margaret, d. Danyell and Ann Haward c	8 ,,	
Marr, Robert, s. Robert and Elizabeth Marr c	14 ,,	
Endeby, John, s. Thomas and Ann Endeby c	15 ,,	
James, Elizabeth, d. Thomas and Elizabeth James c	18 ,,	
Poule, Elizabeth, d. Edward and Mary Poule c	28 ,,	
Parker, { John, Francis, } s. d. William and Mary Parker c	4 Oct.	
Tharrold, James, s. Paul and Alice Tharrold c	6 ,,	
Hames, John, s. Thomas and Mary Hames c	6 ,,	
Cockborn, George, s. George and Elizabeth Cockborn, mercer c	8 ,,	
Markbey, Elizabeth, d. Jonathan and Elizabeth Markbey c	11 ,,	
Gibson, Mary, d. Roger and Mary Gibson c	8 Nov.	

[Fol. 57a.]

Skill, Richard, s. Richard and Ellen Skill c	5 ,,	
Eyre, Thomas, s. Thomas and Elizabeth Eyre c	5 ,,	
Benton, Joan, d. John and Elizabeth Benton c	20 ,,	
Bennett, Frances, d. Martin and Sarah Bennett c	21 ,,	
Cooke, Ann, d. Richard and Margery Cooke c	24 ,,	
Parker, Bridgit, d. Charles and Elizabeth Parker c	26 ,,	
Hamerton, Mary, d. John and Ruth Hamerton c	26 ,,	
Littlebury, Luke, s. Thomas and Grace Littlebury Esqre c	10 Dec.	
Chester, Leonard, s. William and Mary Chester c	22 ,,	
Adison, Mary, d. Thomas and Mary Adison c	22 ,,	
Gibon, Anthony, d. John and Elizabeth Gibon c	5 Jan.	
Curtis, Susanna, d. John and Susanna Curtis c	12 ,,	
Shepherd, Frances, d. Walter and Lucy Shepherd c	16 ,,	
Maccris, Edward, s. John and Elizabeth Maccris c	26 ,,	

Knight, Charles, *s.* Robert and Mary Knight *c*   26 Jan.
Hauley, Elizabeth, *d.* John and Isabel Hauley *c*   26 ,,
Dules, Ralph, *s.* John and Helen Dules *c*   26 ,,
Tuxworth, Stephen, *s.* Stephen and Mary Tuxworth *c*   31 ,,
Bankes, Ann, *d.* John and Elizabeth Bankes *c*   2 Feb.
Slator, Margaret, *d.* Ralph and Margaret Slator *c*   19 ,,
Goodge, Elizabeth, *d.* John and Elizabeth Goodge *c*   20 ,,
Hankock, Joseph, *s.* John and Alice Hankock *c*   25 ,,
Burton, Elizabeth, *d.* Thomas and Ann Burton *c*   16 Mar.

[Fol. 57b.]

MARRIAGES, 1672.

Benton, Thomas }
West, Elizabeth } *m*   15 April

Madison, William }
Burton, Elizabeth } *m*   16 ,,

Curtis, John }
Coates, Susanna } *m*   16 ,,

Clark, William }
Portas, Elizabeth } *m*   16 ,,

Eblewhite, Thomas }
Kennington, Isabell } *m*   27 ,,

Benton, William }
Kerk, Deborah } *m*   7 May

Goodge, John }
Wryton, Elizabeth } *m*   9 ,,

Scamon, Edward }
Houltridge, Prudens } *m*   7 ,,

Kiggs, John }
Nicholls, Susanna } *m*   20 July

Slator, Ralph }
Marshall, Margaret } *m*   21 Aug.

Hauley, Christopher }
Garnes, Mary } *m*   1 Oct.

Laines, Jeremiah }
Enderby, Isabell } *m*   14 Nov.

Martindaile, Robert }
Dixon, Ann } *m*   1 Dec.

Burton, John }
Dodkin, Elizabeth } *m*   14 Jan.

Beverley, Richard }
Pell, Katherine } *m*   7 Mar.

BURIALS, 1672.

Adison, Mary, widow *b*   26 Mar.
Garness, Priscilla, an infant *b*   28 ,,
Gill, Easter, widow *b*   30 ,,
Husey, Thomas, an infant *b*   30 ,,
Hamerton, Auderie, wife Joseph Hamerton *b*   1 April
West, John, translator *b*   4 ,,
Husey, Charles, an infant *b*   13 ,,
Richardson, Elizabeth, wife John Richardson *b*   3 May
Garness, James, mason *b*   13 ,,
Knight, Elizabeth, widow *b*   14 ,,
Smith, Ursilla, widow *b*   17 ,,
Birch, Margaret, wife Thomas Birch *b*   27 ,,
Eland, Mary, wife Hugh Eland *b*   31 ,,
Walsh, Robert, laborer *b*   22 June
Davis, John, a traveller *b*   27 ,,

Tuxworth, Thomas, a young youth *b*	8	July
Douse, Sarah, an infant *b*	28	,,
Aston, William, laborer *b*	12	Aug.
Goodge, Margery, widow *b*	12	,,
Dalles, Lidia, an infant *b*	19	,,
Page, Nicholas, an infant *b*	21	,,
Madison, Elizabeth, wife William Madison *b*	27	,,
Frith, William, an infant *b*	4	Sept.
Houlridge, Ann, widow *b*	10	,,
Frith, Mary, wife William Frith *b*	11	,,

[Fol. 58a.]

Dodkin, Vincent, baker *b*	17	,,
Smith, Alice, Virginis *b*	25	,,
Yates, George, a youth *b*	28	,,
Parker, Mary, wife William Parker *b*	4	Oct.
Martindalle, Sarah, wife Robert Martindaile *b*	4	,,
Burton, John, an infant *b*	6	,,
Bell, Rachel, Virginis *b*	7	,,
Johnson, William, cordwiner *b*	8	,,
Kerk, William, an infant *b*	8	,,
Parker, John, an infant *b*	12	,,
Crastes, Thomas, adolecence *b*	18	,,
Littlebury, Alice, widow *b*	81	,,
Freston, Debora, wife Richard Freston *b*	15	Nov.
Skillan, Richard, an infant *b*	15	,,
Butler, Frances, an infant *b*	17	,,
Bowring, Elizabeth, an infant *b*	22	,,
Broughton, William, an infant *b*	80	,,
Gentile, Bridgit, a young virgin *b*	7	Dec.
Graves, William, an infant *b*	9	,,
Bird, Ann, wife John Bird *b*	9	,,
Perkins, Ann, widow *b*	11	,,
Haward, John, an infant *b*	20	,,
Peares, Ezekiel *b*	22	,,
Parker, Frances, an infant *b*	28	,,
Marley, Joshua, an infant *b*	5	Jan.
Marley, Henry, a young youth *b*	7	,,
Marr, Robert, an infant *b*	12	,,
Kerk, Debora, an infant *b*	15	,,
Poules, Elizabeth, an infant *b*	21	,,
Bradley, John, an infant *b*	24	,,
Knight, Charles, an infant *b*	29	,,
Tharrold, James, an infant *b*	1	Feb.
Hamerton, Susanna, wife Samuell Hamerton *b*	4	,,
Martindalle, Ann, an infant *b*	11	,,
Marshall, Margaret, an infant *b*	20	,,
Chester, John, an infant *b*	4	Mar.
Goodge, Elizabeth, wife John Goodge *b*	6	,,
Tayler, Elizabeth, an infant *b*	28	,,

[Fol. 58b.]

CHRISTENINGS, 1673.

Bonner, Francis, *s.* M^r. Francis and Ann Bonner *c*	2	April
Marley, Joshua, *s.* Joshua Marley deceased *c*	3	,,
Tayler, Richard, *s.* Robert and Helen Tayler *c*	9	,,
Cocker, Edward, *s.* Henry and Elizabeth Cocker *c*	11	,,
Dennis, William, *s.* Richard and Jane Dennis *c*	13	,,
Benton, Ann, *d.* Thomas and Elizabeth Benton *c*	13	,,

— Benton, William, *s.* William and Debora Benton *c*	22 April
Arthera, Martha, *d.* John and Mary Arthera *c*	27 ,,
— Locking, Jane, *d.* Gilbert and Bridget Locking *c*	27 ,,
Pogson, Katherin, *d.* William Pogson *c*	1 May
Browne, Elizabeth, *d.* Jeremiah and Isabell Browne *c*	3 ,,
Riggs, Elizabeth, *d.* John and Susanna Riggs *c*	18 ,,
— Hanam, Steven, *s.* Walter and Ann Hanam, a stranger *c*	25 ,,
Clerk, Elizabeth, *d.* William and Elizabeth Clerk, laborer *c*	6 July
— Wigellsworth, Grant, *s.* Edward and Elizabeth Wigellsworth *c*	13 ,,
Kerk, Ann, *d.* Richard and Ann Kerk *c*	15 ,,
— Husey, Susanna, *d.* John and Susanna Husey, mercer *c*	17 ,,
Madison, William, *s.* Christopher and Elizabeth Madison *c*	18 ,,
— Lawrence, Robert, *s.* of Hollingshead and Elizabeth Lawrence *c*	2 Sept.
Eldred, Anna, *d.* Lydia Eldred *c*	1 Oct.
— Newman, Mary, *d.* John and Ann Newman *c*	5 ,,

[Fol. 59a.]

Broughton, Elizabeth, *d.* John and Mary Broughton *c*	20 ,,
Martindaile, John, *s.* Robert and Ann Martindaile *c*	26 ,,
Gibon, Joseph, *s.* Thomas and James Gibon *c*	2 Nov.
Kerk, Ann, *d.* William and Mary Kerk *c*	2 ,,
Howgrave, John, *s.* Alexander and Elizabeth Howgrave *c*	4 ,,
Willaman, Gilbert, *s.* Gilbert and Grace Willaman *c*	9 ,,
Latherop, Grace, *d.* William and Grace Latherop *c*	13 ,,
Wells, John, *s.* Thomas and Alice Wells, tanner *c*	20 ,,
Scamon, Edward, *s.* Edward and Prudens Scamon *c*	26 ,,
Skill, Faith, *d.* William and Hester Skill *c*	29 ,,
Hauley, Clement, *s.* Christopher and Mary Hauley *c*	30 ,,
Tharrold, Mary, *d.* Paul and Alice Tharrold *c*	7 Dec.
Birch, Elizabeth, *d.* Thomas and Faith Birch *c*	9 ,,
Tharold, Sarah, *d.* John and Dorothy Tharold *c*	14 ,,
Browne, George, *s.* George and Mary Browne *c*	21 ,,
Tayler, Mary, *d.* Francis and Mary Tayler *c*	21 ,,
Goode, Grace, *d.* Thomas and Mary Goode *c*	26 ,,
Haward, John, *s.* Danyell and Ann Haward *c*	1 Jan.
Towill, John, *s.* Edward and Elizabeth Towill *c*	11 ,,
Aspland, William, *s.* John and Bridget Aspland *c*	15 ,,
Shoton, Frances, *d.* Thomas and Susanna Shoton *c*	18 ,,
Osborne, Katherine, *d.* John and Ann Osborne *c*	25 ,,
Beverley, William, *s.* Richard and Katherine Beverley *c*	29 ,,
Markbie, Lidia, *d.* Hastings and Ann Markbie *c*	10 Feb.
Goake, Robert, *s.* John and Elizabeth Goake *c*	16 ,,
Madison, Elizabeth, *d.* William and Elizabeth Madison *c*	23 ,,
Hamerton, John, *s.* John and Ruth Hamerton *c*	24 ,,
Swindall, John, *s.* John and Katherine Swindall *c*	1 Mar.

[Fol. 59b.]

Frith, William, *s.* William and Frances Frith, barber *c*	5 ,,
Blow, Thomas, *s.* George and Judith Blow *c*	10 ,,
Coates, Henry, *s.* Henry and Frances Coates *c*	15 ,,

Here endeth Christenings, 1673.

MARRIAGES, 1673.

Hamerton, Samuel } Brown, Ann } *m*		1 May
Frith, William } Vicars, Frances } *m*		27 ,,
Madison, William } Bradlay, Elizabeth } *m*		27 ,,

Grayson, George } m	17 June	
Westlands, Ann } m		
Freston, Richard } m	14 Aug.	
Gibson, Susannah } m		
Haull, George } m	80 Sept.	
Harrowble, Alice } m		
Aspland, John } m	5 Oct.	
Gelle, Bridgit } m		
Lee, James }	28 ,,	
Pell, Susanna } m		
Parker, William } m	27 Nov.	
Johnson, Ann } m		
Hallam, John } m	27 ,,	
Wells, Margaret } m		
Hamerton, Joseph } m	4 Dec.	
Bromley, Mary } m		
Hamerton, John } m	1 Jan.	
Gaule, Mary } m		
Ouldam, Francis } m	15 ,,	
Bird, Susanna } m		
Kent, William } m	3 Mar.	
Burton, Margaret } m		
Bird, John } m	5 ,,	
Dannol, Ann } m		

BURIALLS, 1678.

Tayler, Joyes b	80 ,,	
Leverloke, John, a young youth b	2 April	
Marley, Joshua, an infant b	5 ,,	
Randes, Dorothy, widow b	7 ,,	
Martindalle, Christopher b	17 ,,	
Benton, Elizabeth, an infant b	28 ,,	
Marley, Elizabeth, an infant b	5 May	
Butler, Joseph b	6 ,,	
Burton, Elizabeth, an infant b	19 June	
Carlton, John, a strainger b	20 ,,	
Tunstall, Edmund, an infant b	1 Aug.	
Arther, John, a laborer b	8 ,,	
Benton, Ann, an infant b	10 ,,	
Clerk, Elizabeth, an infant b	18 ,,	
Walton, Phillip, a strainger b	20 ,,	
Tayler, William, a felmonger b	9 Sept.	
Husey, Susanna, an infant b	18 ,,	
Madison, William, an infant b	20 ,,	
Kerk, William, an infant b	8 Oct.	
Joanes, Simon, Bucher b	4 Nov.	
Broughton, Mary, an infant b	10 ,,	
Willaman, Gilbert, an infant b	20 ,,	
Perkins, Katherine, Widow b	80 ,,	
Skill, Faith, an infant b	7 Dec.	
Hanam, Steaven, an infant b	9 ,,	

[Fol. 60a.]

Thompson, Richard, a youth b	18 ,,	
Grenfield, Martha, a virgin b	23 ,,	
Forman, Susanna, Widow b	7 Jan.	
Haward, John, an infant b	10 ,,	
Simpson, Ellen, a young virgin b	16 ,,	

— Laines, Sarah, wife William Laines *b*	26	Jan.
—James, Thomas, draper *b*	26	,,
—Howbie, William, yeoman *b*	27	,,
—Houlderness, John, yeoman *b*	27	,,
— Swindall, Elizabeth, an infant *b*	11	Feb.
- Madison, Elizabeth, an infant *b*	25	,,
—Perkins, Robert, Glover *b*	2	Mar.
—Clapam, Mary, wife Ralp Clapam *b*	2	,,
—Armsbie, Robert, a young youth *b*	6	,,
— Lamingman, Robert, an infant *b*	9	,,
· Aspland, William, an infant *b*	10	,,
—Beverley, William, an infant *b*	19	,,
— Elston, George, Tayler *b*	20	,,

CHRISTENINGS, 1674.

—Tayler, Priscilla, *d.* William and Ann Tayler, felmonger *c*	26	,,
— Douse, Thomas, *s.* Thomas and Elizabeth Douse *c*	29	,,
—Lettis, John, *s.* Richard and —— Lettis *c*	5	April
—Dixon, Elizabeth, *d.* John and Elizabeth Dixon, carier *c*	19	,,
—Parker, Jane, *d.* Charles and Elizabeth Parker *c*	20	,,
—Gentile, Benjamin, *s.* Benjamin and Elizabeth Gentile *c*	26	,,
—Groume, Ann, *d.* Thomas and Esthe Groume *c*	17	May
—Freston, Elizabeth, *d.* Mr. Thomas and Grace Freston *c*	22	,,
— Benton, William, *s.* William and Debora Benton *c*	24	,,
—Grayson, Joshua, *s.* George and Ann Grayson *c*	24	,,
—Houilridg, Sarah, *d.* Richard and Ann Houilridg *c*	17	June
— Dixon, Richard, *s.* Thomas and Anne Dixon *c*	17	,,
— Mainwell, Ann, *d.* John and Ann Mainwell *c*	20	,,
—Houmes, Richard, *s.* Thomas and Amey Houmes *c*	28	,,
—Tayler, James, *s.* Robert and Hester Tayler *c*	5	July
—Knight, Mary, *d.* Robert and Mary Knight *c*	14	Aug.
—Cockborn, Susanna, *d.* George and Elizabeth Cockborn, mercer *c*	18	,,
—Westeble, Katherine, *d.* William and Sarah Westebie *c*	23	,,
—Page, Matthew, *s.* Thomas and Frances Page *c*	24	,,
—Hauley, { Mary, Ellin, } *dd.* John and Isabel Hauley *c*	2	Sept.
—Redthorne, Elizabeth, *d.* Thomas and Ann Redthorne *c*	18	,,
—Marley, Edward, *s.* Jonathan and Elizabeth Marley *c*	19	,,

[Fol. 60b.]

—Hanam, Robert, *s.* Walter and Ann Hanam *c*	21	,,
—Graves, Elizabeth, *d.* William and Margery Graves *c*	31	,,
—Ronoth, Elizabeth, *d.* Edward and Judith Ronoth *c*	6	Oct.
—Freston, Richard, *s.* Richard and Susanna Freston *c*	8	,,
—Riggs, Margaret, *d.* John and Susanna Riggs *c*	18	,,
—Bennet, Frances, *d.* Martin and Sarah Bennet *c*	22	,,
—Ranby, John, *s.* John and Mary Ranby *c*	1	Nov.
—Clark, Elizabeth, *d.* William and Elizabeth Clark, laborer *c*	8	,,
— Burton, William, *s.* Thomas and Ann Burton *c*	15	,,
- Looking, Gilbert, *s.* Gilbert and Bridget Looking *c*	15	,,
—Slater, Ellin, *d.* Ralph and Margaret Slater *c*	17	,,
- Bichfield, John, *s.* John and Ann Bichfield *c*	10	Jan.
—Pogson, William, *s.* William and —— Pogson, Baker *c*	18	,,
—Benton, Thomas, *s.* Thomas and Elizabeth Benton *c*	31	,,
—Budivant, Mary, *d.* John and Christine Budivant *c*	31	,,
- Aspland, John, *s.* John and Bridget Aspland *c*	3	Feb.
—Cocker, John, *s.* Henry and Elizabeth Cocker *c*	4	,,
— Markby, William, *s.* William and Ann Markby *c*	9	,,
— Fielding, Joseph, *s.* Thomas and Mary Fielding *c*	19	,,

—Wigellsworth, Edward, *s.* Edward and Elizabeth Wigellsworth *c* 24 Feb.
—Bird, Richard, *s.* John and Anna Bird *c* 25 ,,
—Garland, Ann, *d.* Robert and Isabell Garland *c* 7 Mar.
—Bonner, Frances, *d.* Mr. Francis and Ann Bonner *c* 9 ,,
—Thew, Susanna, *d.* George and Katherin Thew, carpenter *c* 11 ,,
—Gibson, Edward, *s.* Roger and Mary Gibson *c* 14 ,,
—Husey, William, *s.* John and Susanna Husey *c* 17 ,,
—Smith, Gilbert, *s.* Thomas and Elizabeth Smith, mason *c* 21 ,,
—Vinter, Henry, *s.* John and —— Vinter, glover *c* 21 ,,

[Fol. 61*a*.]

Marriages, 1674.

—Richardson, John ⎱ *m*
— Drury, Mary ⎰ 7 May
— Fielding, Thomas ⎱ *m*
—Wigellsworth, Mary ⎰ 7 ,,
—Garland, Robert ⎱ *m*
—Robison, Isabel ⎰ 14 ,,
—Bottomley, William ⎱ *m*
— Bird, Elizabeth ⎰ 21 ,,
— North, Thomas ⎱ *m*
— Prince, Ann ⎰ 26 ,,
—Burton, Latherop ⎱ *m*
—Leach, Alice ⎰ 5 Juiy
— Willie, Henry ⎱ *m*
—Bowering, Elizabeth ⎰ 23 ,,
— Preston, Thomas ⎱ *m*
— Madens, Margaret ⎰ 3 Dec.

Burialls, 1674.

— Perkins, Mary, a young virgin *b* 26 Mar
—Jeokells, Ann, a young virgin *b* 28 ,,
— Dawson, Mary, a virgin *b* 28 ,,
— Tayler, Mary, an infant *b* 80 ,,
—Freston, Thomas, an infant *b* 5 April
— Goudge, Grace, an infant *b* 11 ,,
—Shepley, William, gent *b* 14 ,,
—Lamaman, Elizabeth, an infant *b* 16 ,,
—Bennet, Frances, an infant *b* 15 May
— Cooke, Ann, an infant *b* 15 ,,
—Joanes, widow *b* 80 ,,
—Adison, Mary, an infant *b* 3 June
—Tayler, James, an infant *b* 8 July
—James, Thomas, an infant *b* 9 ,,
— Maccaris, John, felmonger *b* 26 ,,
— Grayson, Joshua, an infant *b* 10 Aug.
— Bonner, Thomas, an infant *b* 24 ,,
—Curtis, John, an infant *b* 19 Sept.
— Redthorn, Elizabeth, an infant *b* 19 ,,
— Thew, Katherine, an infant *b* 28 ,,
—Graves, Elizabeth, an infant *b* 5 Oct.
— Freston, Susanna, wife Richard Freston *b* 10 ,,
— Rouoth, Elizabeth, an infant *b* 10 ,,
— Freston, Richard, an infant *b* 18 ,,
— Moltby, Elizabeth, wife William Moltby *b* 8 Nov.
—Tothby, Robert, tanner *b* 7 ,,
—Bonner, Francis, an infant *b* 7 ,,
—Curtis, Ann, wife John Curtis *b* 15 ,,
—Moltby, William, laborer *b* 24 ,,
— Dixon, Richard, an infant *b* 26 ,,

Narter, Mary, a virgin *b*	5 Dec.
Gysing, Elizabeth, wife George Gysing *b*	30 ,,
Clarke, Elizabeth, an infant *b*	6 Jan.
Douse, Elizabeth, wife Thomas Douse *b*	7 ,,
Gibson, Jane, wife M^r. Thomas Gibson } *b* Vicar of Horncastle }	17 ,,
Douse, Thomas, an infant *b*	20 ,,
Page, Thomas *b*	26 ,,
Benton, Thomas, an infant *b*	2 Feb.
Aspland, Bridgit, wife Thomas Aspland *b*	8 ,,
Mackeris, Bridgit, wife Thomas Mackeris *b*	12 ,,
Fielding, Joseph, an infant *b*	20 ,,
Richardson, Elizabeth, widow *b*	27 ,,
Frith, Ann, an infant *b*	9 Mar.

[Fol. 61*b*.]

CHRISTENINGS, 1675.

Hamerton, George, *s*. John and Mary Hamerton *c*	1 April
Bruton, John, *s*. John and Mary Bruton *c*	4 ,,
Curtis, Esther, *d*. John and Jane Curtis *c*	11 ,,
Madison, Elizabeth, *d*. Christopher and Elizabeth Madison *c*	20 ,,
Harcome, Thomas, *s*. John and Lidia Harcome *c*	25 ,,
Harrison, Elizabeth, *d*. Robert and Elizabeth Harrison *c*	25 ,,
Lamaman, Mary, *d*. Robert and Elizabeth Lamaman *c*	25 ,,
Gunis, William, *s*. William and Mary Gunis *c*	1 May
Hamerton, Robert, *s*. Thomas and Ann Hamerton, glover *c*	4 ,,
Burton, Luke, *s*. Nathaniel and Alice Burton *c*	24 ,,
Willie, Elizabeth, *d*. Henry and Elizabeth Willie *c*	9 ,,
North, John, *s*. Thomas and —— North, apoticary *c*	11 ,,
Hughison, Elizabeth, *d*. John and Mary Hughison *c*	25 ,,
Poule, Mary, *d*. Edward and Mary Poule *c*	30 ,,
Beverley, George, *s*. George and Anna Beverley *c*	8 June
Leach, Esther, *d*. Timothy and Elizabeth Leach *c*	9 ,,
Forman, Jeffery, *s*. Andrew Elin Forman *c*	24 ,,
Grasen, Richard, *s*. George and Ann Grasen *c*	27 ,,
Dannet, Peter, *s*. William and Mary Dannet *c*	4 July
Bradlay, Elizabeth, *d*. Henry and Mary Bradlay *c*	10 ,,
Hamerton, Bromley, *s*. Joseph and Mary Hamerton *c*	23 ,,
Browne, Christopher, *s*. Jeremiah and Isabele Browne *c*	8 Aug.
Birch, Susanna, *d*. Thomas and Faith Birch *c*	9 ,,
Wright, Elizabeth, *d*. Richard and Alia Wright *c*	12 ,,
Ouldam, Mary, *d*. Francis and Susanna Ouldam *c*	15 ,,
Scaman, Judith, *d*. Edward and Prudens Scaman *c*	30 ,,
Kerk, Francis, *d*. Richard and Ann Kerk *c*	1 Sept.
Howard, Danyell, *s*. Danyell and Ann Howard *c*	5 ,,
Danks, Elizabeth, *d*. Edward and Mary Danks *c*	5 ,,
Parks, Charles, *s*. Charles and Elizabeth Parks *c*	19 ,,
Martindaile, Robert, *s*. Robert and Ann Martindaile *c*	26 ,,

[Fol. 62*a*.]

Kent, Mary, *d*. William and Mary Kent, candler *c*	28 ,,
Chester, Henry, *s*. William and Mary Chester *c*	10 Oct.
Tayler, William, *s*. William and Ann Tayler, fellmonger *c*	14 ,,
Edenstow, Francis, *s*. Richard and Ann Edenstow *c*	8 Nov.
Grave, Samuell, *s*. William and Margery Grave *c*	11 ,,
Hollinghedg, Thomas *s*. —— and Elizabeth Hollinghedg, tanner *c*	18 ,,
Goudge, Frances, *d*. Thomas and Mary Goudge *c*	25 ,,
Skill, Faith, *d*. William and Hellen Skill *c*	6 Dec.
Goake, Joseph, *s*. John and Elizabeth Goake *c*	7 ,,

- Ferford, Mary, d. John and Ellen Ferford, a strainger c   14 Dec
- Gibon, Elizabeth, d. John and Ann Gibon c   18 ,,
- Broughton, Joan, d. Robert and Alice Broughton c   20 ,,
- Browne, Elizabeth, d. George and Mary Browne c   1 Jan.
- Bankes, Robert, s. John and Elizabeth Bankes c   16 ,,
- Preston, William, s. Thomas and Mary Preston c   16 ,,
- Freston, Grace, d. Mr. Thomas and Grace Freston c   17 ,,
- Hancock, Steaven, s. John and Alice Hancock c   2 Feb.
- Gibon, John, s. John and Francis Gibon c   4 ,,
- Hann, Andrew, s. John and Alice Hann c   6 ,,
- Howes, Anthony, s. Thomas and Amey Howes c   13 ,,
- Cocker, Ellen, d. Henry and Elizabeth Cocker c   25 ,,
- Scotterick, Frances, d. John and Hellen Scotterick c   26 ,,
- Clark, George, s. William and Elizabeth Clark, laborer c   5 Mar.
- Denis, Elizabeth, d. Richard and Jane Denis c   5 ,,
- Hamerton, William, s. John and Ruth Hamerton c   6 ,,
- Wells, Benjamin, s. Thomas and Alice Wells c   7 ,,
- Haulley, Francis, s. Christopher and Mary Haulley c   15 ,,

[Fol. 62b.]

MARRIAGES, 1675.

- Wray, William } m   6 May
- Dixon, Ann
- Curtis, John } m   6 ,,
- Knight, Ann
- Scotterick, John } m   31 ,,
- Bocock, Hellen
- Aspland, John } m   24 June
- Foster, Ann
- Tayler, George } m   6 July
- Staines, Mary
- Croft, John } m   10 Feb.
- Clarke, Susanna

BURIALS, 1675.

- Hanam, Robert, an infant b   25 Mar.
- Collings, Ralph, an infant b   30 ,,
- Houmes, John, an infant b   4 April
- Clapham, Robert, a youth b   8 ,,
- Boulton, George b   17 ,,
- Gooderick, Deborah, wife of William Gooderick, of Stickney b   28 ,,
- Lamaman, Mary, an infant b   4 May
- Willie, Elizabeth, an infant b   11 ,,
- Nicholdson, John, pinder b   30 ,,
- Greene, Ann, widow b   5 June
- Redthorne, Thomas b   8 ,,
- Hauley, Mary, an infant b   26 ,,
- Bird, Richard, an infant b   28 ,,
- West, Ann, widow b   20 July
- Hamerton, Bromley, an infant b   26 ,,
- Peares, John, an infant b   28 ,,
- Francis, Elizabeth, a virgin b   31 ,,
- Wright, Elizabeth, an infant b   15 Aug.
- Dannol, Mary, an infant b   24 ,,
- Bird, John, an infant b   5 Sept.
- Clarke, Sarah, wife Henry Clarke b   12 Oct.
- Burton, Luke, an infant b   14 ,,
- Chester, Henry, an infant b   14 ,,

Bernard, Martha, a young virgin *b*	5 Nov.
Edenstow, Francis, an infant *b*	14 ,,
Dixlson, William, Esq., departed life Nov. 10th, and was imbalmed here until	21 ,,
Grason, Margaret, a widow *b*	28 ,,
Shotten, Susanna, a young virgin *b*	29 ,,
Tharrold, Margaret, widow *b*	1 Dec.
Husey, M^{rs}. Ellen, widow *b*	21 ,,
White, Thomas, weaver *b*	27 ,,
Heath, M^r. Richard, draper *b*	25 Jan.
Gibson, Edward, an infant *b*	28 ,,
Smith, William, of Tellbie *b*	1 Feb.
Gibon, John, an infant *b*	7 ,,
Chamberlaine, John, adolesence *b*	,,
Skotterlok, Darris, an infant *b*	3 Mar.
Hamerton, William, an infant *b*	8 ,,

[Fol. 68*a*.]

CHRISTENINGS, 1676.

Bird, Ann, *d.* John and Ann Bird *c*	26 ,,
Dailes, Ruth, *d.* John and Hellen Dailes *c*	26 ,,
Tayler, James, *s.* Robert and Hellen Tayler, fellmonger *c*	27 ,,
Madison, George, *s.* William and Elizabeth Madison *c*	29 ,,
Cockborne, Charles, *s.* George and Elizabeth Cockborne, mercer *c*	29 ,,
Towill, Mildred, *d.* Edward and Elizabeth Towill *c*	31 ,,
Mainwell, Mary, *d.* John and Ann Mainwell *c*	15 April
Colling, Elizabeth, *d.* Thomas and Alice Colling *c*	16 ,,
Markbey, Henry, *s.* Jonatban and Elizabeth Markbey *c*	18 ,,
Markbie, Mary, *d.* Hastens and Ann Markbie *c*	19 ,,
Dixon, Sara, *d.* John and Elizabeth Dixon, carrier *c*	20 ,,
Fidling, Thomas, *s.* Thomas and Mary Fidling *c*	23 ,,
Tharrold, Edward, *s.* Saul and Alice Tharrold *c*	28 ,,
Coates, Thomas, *s.* Henry and Frances Coates *c*	27 ,,
Gathorp, Frances, *d.* William and Grace Gathorp *c*	27 ,,
Tharrold, Abigail, *d.* John and Dorothy Tharrold *c*	7 May
Marr, Robert, *s.* Robert and Elizabeth Marr *c*	7 ,,
Shotten, Charles, *s.* Thomas and Susanna Shotten *c*	15 ,,
Buxton, Mary, *d.* Nathaniel and Alice Buxton *c*	11 June
Willie, John, *s.* Henry and Elizabeth Willie *c*	11 ,,
Husey, Ellenor, *d.* John and Susanna Husey, mercer *c*	15 ,,
Tuxwoth, Mary, *d.* Steven and ——— Tuxwoth *c*	16 July
Curtis, Robert, *s.* John and Ann Curtis, laborer *c*	28 ,,
Ridgge, Mary, *d.* John and Susanna Ridgge *c*	30 ,,
Simpson, William, *s.* John and Elizabeth Simpson *c*	21 Aug.
Gentile, William, *s.* Benjamin and Elizabeth Gentile *c*	20 Sept.
Broughton, William, *s.* John and ——— Broughton *c*	1 Oct.
Pogson, Samuel, *s.* William and ——— Pogson, baker *c*	1 ,,
Maccaris, Thomas, *s.* John and Elizabeth Maccaris *c*	8 ,,
Bichfield, Thomas, *s.* John and Ann Bichfield *c*	8 ,,

[Fol. 68*b*.]

Minting, Edward, *s.* Richard and Elizabeth Minting *c*	15 ,,
Clark, Amey, *d.* Henry and Sarah Clark *c*	8 Nov.
Benton, Richard, *s.* William and Debora Benton *c*	15 ,,
Locking, Brigit, *d.* Gilbert and Brigit Locking *c*	19 ,,
Swindall, Robert, *s.* Robert and Katherine Swindall *c*	19 ,,
Hamerton, Audery, *d.* Joseph and Mary Hamerton *c*	11 Dec.
Littlebury, Grace, *d.* Thomas and Grace Littlebury, draper *c*	19 ,,
Wigellsworth, John, *s.* Edward and Elizabeth Wigellsworth *c*	21 ,,

Madison, Thomas, *s.* William and Mary Madison, Jr. *c*   24 Dec.
Kerk, Richard, *s.* Richard and Ann Kerk, butcher *c*   24 „
Birch, Dorcas, *d.* Thomas and Faith Birch, tanner *c*   26 „
Tayler, Francis, *s.* Francis and Mary Tayler, glover *c*   1 Jan.
Gibon, John, *s.* Thomas and Jane Gibon, mason *c*   1 „
Beverley, Thomas, *s.* Mr. George and Anna Beverley *c*   2 „
Budivant, William, *s.* John and —— Budivant *c*   14 „
Bonner, Thomas, *s.* Mr. Francis and Ann Bonner *c*   18 „
Edenstow, Richard, *s.* Richard and Ann Edenstow *c*   19 „
Bennet, Martin, *s.* Martin and Sarah Bennet *c*   6 Feb.
Hamerton, Elizabeth, *d.* Mr. John and Mary Hamerton, tanner *c*   8 „
Hauley, Alice, *d.* John and Isabell Hauley *c*   25 „
Goughe, Mary, *d.* Samuel and Elizabeth Goughe, taylor *c*   25 „
North, Thomas, *s.* Thomas and Ann North, anapothicary *c*   1 Mar.
Foster, Elizabeth, *d.* Nathaniel and Dorothy Foster *c*   4 „
Perkins, Thomas, *s.* Thomas and Alice Perkins, tanner *c*   18 „
Gibson, Edward, *s.* Roger and Mary Gibson *c*   24 „

[Fol. 64a.]

MARRIAGES, 1676.

West, Francis } *m*   29 Mar.
Diton, Elizabeth }

Freston, Richard } *m*   27 April
Marley, Judith }

Psudle, Samuel } *m*   30 „
Hudleston, Elizabeth }

Elsey, Edward } *m*   25 May
Walker, Alice }

Doules, Thomas } *m*   25 „
Jacson, Francis }

White, Thomas } *m*   25 „
Hart, Ann }

Waterman, Thomas } *m*   11 July
Wilaman, Mary }

Wright, Thomas } *m*   18 Oct.
Hareble, Mary }

Thomson, Richard } *m*   16 Nov.
Simpson, Elizabeth }

BURIALS, 1676.

Madison, George, infant *b*   31 Mar.
Gouldsborw, William *b*   7 April
Bird, Ann, an infant *b*   9 „
Tharrold, Edward, an infant *b*   25 „
Dixon, Sarah, an infant *b*   30 „
Wilaman, Gilbert, shoemaker *b*   2 May
Marley, Henry, an infant *b*   4 „
Tayler, James, an infant *b*   6 „
Lawrence, Thomas, an infant *b*   26 „
Tayler, Prisilla, an infant *b*   10 June
Cocker, Hellen, an infant *b*   23 „
Butler, Elizabeth, widow *b*   6 Aug.
Gibon, Thomas, a youth *b*   13 „
Tharrold, Jane, a young virgin *b*   17 „
Simpson, William, an infant *b*   22 „
Burton, William, an infant *b*   26 „
Simpson, John, laboror *b*   30 „
Pacey, Elizabeth, wife Benjamin Pacey *b*   8 Sept.
Wigellsworth, Samuel *b*   13 „

Bradlay, Henry, shoemaker *b*	28 Sept.
Hudson, Mary, spinster *b*	21 Oct.
Clark, Amey, an infant *b*	18 Nov.
Maccaris, Edward, farmer *b*	18 ,,
Rouoth, Edward, shoemaker *b*	14 Dec.
Keark, Mary, spinster *b*	19 ,,
Hamerton, Audery, an infant *b*	21 ,,
Wigellsworth, John, an infant *b*	22 ,,
Madens, Margery, widow *b*	5 Jan.
Tayler, Ann, a young virgin *b*	10 ,,
Edenstow, Richard, an infant *b*	25 ,,
Perkins, Elizabeth, a young virgin *b*	30 ,,
Enderbie, Thomas, tayler *b*	5 Feb.
Hanley, Alice, an infant *b*	9 Mar.
Gentile, Elizabeth, wife of Benjamin Gentile *b*	23 ,,
Couper, William of Housam, cutler *b*	28 ,,

[Fol. 64*b*.]

CHRISTENINGS, 1677.

West, Edmund, *s.* Francis and Elizabeth West *c*	27 Mar.
White, John, *s.* Thomas and Ann White, weaver *c*	1 April
Leach, Mary, *d.* Timothy and Elizabeth Leach *c*	1 ,,
Martindaile, Mary, *d.* Robert and Ann Martindaile *c*	15 ,,
Elsey, Ann, *d.* Edward and Alice Elsey *c*	26 ,,
Douse, John, *s.* Thomas and Francis Douse *c*	6 May
Adison, Francis, *s.* Thomas and Mary Adison *c*	27 ,,
Ranby, Elizabeth, *d.* John and Mary Ranby *c*	3 June
Bird, Elizabeth, *d.* John and Ann Bird *c*	6 ,,
Husey, Sarah, *d.* John and Susanna Husey *c*	8 ,,
Curtis, John, *s.* John and Ann Curtis *c*	17 ,,
Hollingshead, Elizabeth, *d.* Lawrance and Elizabeth Hollingshead *c*	18 ,,
Marley, George, son of Jonathan and Elizabeth Marley *c*	23 ,,
Notingham, Hannah, *d.* Mʳ. Richard and Dinah Notingham *c*	1 July
Chester, Honey, *d.* William and Mary Chester *c*	8 ,,
Cockburn, Benjamin, *s.* George and Elizabeth Cockburn *c*	16 ,,
Hamerton, Thomas, *s.* Thomas and Ann Hamerton *c*	22 ,,
Aer [? Eyre], Robert, *s.* Thomas and Elizabeth Aer *c*	4 Aug.
Tayler, George, *s.* Robert and Ellen Tayler *c*	5 ,,
Lamewell, Nathaniel, *s.* Robert and Elizabeth Lamewell *c*	26 Sept.
Preston, Elizabeth, *d.* Thomas and Margaret Preston *c*	30 ,,
Markby, Elizabeth, *d.* William and Ann Markby *c*	2 Oct.
Parker, Robert, *s.* Charles and Elizabeth Parker *c*	3 ,,
Wright, George, *s.* Thomas and Mary Wright *c*	7 ,,

[Fol. 65*a*.]

BURIALS, 1677.

Harison, Elizabeth, an infant *b*	21 April
Shotten, Edward, an infant *b*	22 ,,
Martindaile, Mary, an infant *b*	12 May
Tayler, Ann, *d.* William Tayler, tanner *b*	16 ,,
Elson, Alice, wife of Edward Elson *b*	21 ,,
Richaison, Elizabeth *b*	26 ,,
Cortas, Susannah, wife of John Cortas *b*	7 July
Carlton, Elizabeth, *d.* John and Jane Carlton *b*	19 ,,
Hamerton, Thomas, *s.* Thomas and Ann Hamerton, junior *b*	31 ,,
Aer, Robert, *s.* Thomas and Elizabeth Aer *b*	7 Aug.
Coates, John, *s.* John and Ann Coates *b*	2 Sept.
Leach, Mary, *d.* Thomas and Elizabeth Leach *b*	6 ,,

- Freston, Grace, M^{rs}. wife M^r. Thomas Freston b ... 15 Sept.
- Broughton, Johney, d. Robert and Alice Broughton b ... 17 ,,
- Thewe, Mary, M^{rs}. b ... 17 ,,
- Cortas, Robert b ... 25 ,,
- Knight, Mary, d. Robert and Mary Knight b ... 27 ,,
- Wright, George, s. Thomas and Mary Wright b ... 9 Oct.
- Marlay, George, s. Jonathan and Elizabeth Marlay b ... 11 ,,

MARRIAGES, 1677.

- Mackris, Thomas } m ... 25 April
- Routh, Judith
- Pacey, Joseph } m ... 26 ,,
- Willams, Elizabeth
- Gentell, Benjamin } m ... 2 May
- Jackson, Sarah
- Attkinson, William } m ... 7 June
- Maner, Margery
- Gentell, Thomas } m ... 20 ,,
- Pacey, Elizabeth
- Pasey, Timothy } m ... 31 July
- Nickolls, Jane

BURIALS, from ye 15th of October, 1677, to 25th March, 1678.

- Watson, William b ... 1 Nov.
- Teasdale, Robert b ... 9 ,,
- Breeton, Ann, wife of William Breeton b ... 15 ,,
- Lands, Margaret, d. William Lands b ... 9 Dec.
- Frith, William b ... 13 ,,

CHRISTENINGS, from the 15th October, 1677, to the 25th March, 1678.

- Wells, Rachel, d. Thomas and Alice Wells c ... 19 Dec.
- Goake, Francis, s. John and Elizabeth Goake c ... 22 ,,
- Allison, Allen, s. Gilbert and Jane Allison c ... 5 Jan.
- Lathorne, Thomas, s. William and Grace Lathorne c ... 12 Feb.

[Fol. 65b.]

- Richier, Bridget, d. Peter and Sarah Richier, doctor of physicke c ... 19 ,,
- Oldham, Frances, d. Francis Oldham c ... 29 ,,
- Pasey, William, s. Joseph and Elizabeth Pasey c ... 25 ,,
- Scaman, Ann, d. Edward and Prudens Scaman c ... 16 Mar.
- Dawe, William, s. William and Markby Dawe c ... 20 ,,
- Hamerton, Mary, d. Joseph and Mary Hamerton, junior c ... 23 ,,
- Madison, Mary, d. Christopher and Elizabeth Madison c ... 23 ,,

CHRISTENINGS, 1678.

- Gentle, Timothy, s. Benjamin and Sarah Gentle c ... 25 Mar.
- Richardson, Ann, d. John and Mary Richardson c ... 28 ,,
- Mackeriss, Thomas, s. Thomas and Judith Mackeriss c ... 23 June
- Clarke, Henry, s. Henry and Sarah Clarke c ... 9 July
- Leach, Mary, d. Timothy and Elisabeth Leach c ... 7 Aug.
- Broughton, Alice, d. Robert and Alice Broughton c ... 12 ,,
- Burton, Luke, s. Nathaniel and Alice Burton, draper c ... 19 ,,
- Buddivant, Edward, a bastard son of Ann Buddivant c ... 1 Sept.
- Wright, Susanna, d. Richard and Alice Wright c ... 3 ,,
- Bitchfield, Samuel, s. John and Ann Bitchfield c ... 7 ,,
- Markby, Elizabeth, d. John and Ann Markby c ... 15 ,,
- Hamerton, Susanna, d. John and Mary Hamerton, junr. c ... 25 ,,
- Freston, Judith, d. Richard and Judith Freston c ... 22 Oct.

North, Elizabeth, *d.* Thomas and Ann North *c*   22 Oct.
Preston, Jane, *d.* Thomas and Mary Preston *c*   24 ,,

[Fol. 66a.]

Hamerton, Thomas, *s.* William and Elizabeth Hamerton *c*   28 ,,
Pogson, John, *s.* William and Elizabeth Pogson *c*   17 Nov.
Tuxworth, Frances, *d.* Stephen and Mary Tuxworth *c*   7 Jan.
Oldham, Frances, *d.* Francis and Susanna Oldham *c*   9 ,,
Pasey, William, *s.* Joseph and Elizabeth Pasey *c*   14 ,,
Hawkley, Ann, *d.* Christopher and Mary Hawkley *c*   16 ,,
Locking, Ann, *d.* Gilbert and Bridgett Locking *c*   23 ,,
Birch, Obadiah, *s.* Thomas and Faith Birch *c*   28 Feb.
Benton, {John Anne} *s.d.* William and Deborah Benton *c*   13 ,,
Danks, Philip, *s.* Edward and Alice Danks *c*   13 ,,
Cockborne, Philip, *s.* George and Elizabeth Cockborne *c*   14 ,,
Rolleston, Godfrey, *s.* Godfrey and Ann Rolleston *c*   24 ,,
Baudricke, Cyriac, *s.* Thomas and Mary Bawdricke *c*   28 ,,
Knight, Mary, *d.* Robert and Mary Knight *c*   1 Mar.
Downes, Elizabeth, *d.* Samuel and Elizabeth Downes *c*   11 ,,
Goake, Elizabeth, *d.* John and Elizabeth Goake *c*   12 ,,

MARRIAGES, 1678.

Martindale, Christopher } *m*
Alesby, Elizabeth   25 May
Cater, John } *m*
Huddleston, Frances   12 June
Carre, John } *m*
Gibson, Mary   25 Aug.
Beeton, William } *m*
Croft, Amy   11 Sept.
Gentle, Benjamin } *m*
Bonner, Elizabeth   11 Jan.

[Fol. 66b].

BURYALLS, 1678.

Curtis, Robert, labourer *b*   27 Mar.
Nottingham, Richard, gent. *b*   30 Mar.
Frith, William, barber *b*   5 April
Holmes, Edward, labourer *b*   14 ,,
Kirke, Richard, *s.* Richard Kirke *b*   16 ,,
Gibson, Thomas, vicar [of Horncastle] *b*   22 ,,
Nicholls, Thomas, carpenter *b*   25 May
Benton, John, *s.* William Benton, labourer *b*   17 June
Wharse, James, *s.* James Wharse, cutler *b*   23 ,,
Richard, Bridget, *d.* Robert Richard, Dr. of Physick *b*   3 July
Curtis, Susanna, wife John Curtis, labourer *b*   9 ,,
Curtis, Esther, *d.* John Curtis, labourer *b*   17 ,,
Curtis, John, *s.* John Curtis, labourer *b*   28 ,,
Leach, Mary, *d.* Timothy and Elizabeth Leach *b*   8 Aug.
Malley, John, *s.* John and Isabel Malley *b*   9 ,,
Broughton, Mary, *d.* John and Mary Broughton, glover *b*   12 ,,
Westerby, Katherine, *d.* William and Sarah Westerby, painter *b*   14 ,,
Davison, Mary, *d.* of Thomas and Mary Davison, cordwainer *b*   16 ,,
Goud, Samuel, tayler *b*   20 ,,
Cater, John, *s.* Richard and Mary Cater, tallow chandler *b*   20 ,,
Mackaris, Thomas, *s.* John Mackaris, tanner *b*   27 ,,
Lanes, William, tayler *b*   2 Sept.
Markby, Elizabeth, *d.* Johnathan Markby, powterer *b*   2 ,,

Tuxworth, Mary, d. Stephen Tuxworth, cordwainer b   6 Sept.
Ury, David, s. Thomas and Mary Ury, junior b   6 ,,
Hussey, Susan, d. John and Susan Hussey, mercer b   15 ,,
Hamerton, Margery, widow b   20 ,,
Waterfall, Bridget, w. Richard Waterfall b   7 Oct.
Cocker, Henry, saddler b   13 ,,
Clarke, Anthonie, cordwainer b   14 ,,
Beverley, Ann, w. George Beverley, clerke b   18 ,,
Tomson, Robert, s. Robt. and Elizabeth Tomson b   20 ,,
Westerby, Katherine, widow b   22 ,,
Markby, Hastings, butcher b   22 ,,
Gentle, Sarah, w. Benjamin Gentle, labourer b   24 ,,
Markham, Thomas, s. John and Lydia Markham b   25 ,,
Bonner, William, labourer b   27 ,,
Carre, Thomas, singleman b   28 ,,
Stubbs, Ellen, widow b   4 Nov.
Bonner, * * s. Francis Bonner, clerke b   4 ,,

[Fol. 67a].

BURIALS, 1679.

Farrow, John, s. John and Dorothy Farrow b   4 Sept.
Menwell, Thomas, s. John and Elizabeth Menwell ? b   4 Oct.

1681.

North, Henry, s. Thomas North, apothecary c   16 Aug.

    *   *   *
    *   *   *
    *   *   *
    *   *   *
    *   *   *

Tuxworth, Thomas, s. Stephen and Mary Tuxworth c   30 May

1682.

Halley, Christopher, s. Christopher and Mary Halley c   17 April
Daukes, Edward, s. Edward Daukes c   19 ,,
Daukes, Thomas, s. Edward Daukes c   19 ,,
Westel, Christopher, s. Thomas and Ann Westel c   20 Mar.
Clark, Henry, s. Henry and Sarah Clark c   25 ,,
Menwell, Rose, d. John and Elizabeth Menwell c   15 May

1683.

Bitchfield, Mary, d. Thomas and Mary Bitchfield c   22 April
Anderson, Thomas, s. William and Bridget Anderson c   25 ,,
Lodington, Mary, d. Thomas and Mary Lodington, Vicar of
    Horncastle c   30 ,,
Tuxworth, Ann, d. Stephen and Mary Tuxworth c   15 Aug.
Leach, John, s. Richard and Catherine Leach c   13 Oct.
Atkinson, Mary, d. William and Margery Atkinson c   31 ,,
Richison, Henry, s. Henry and Alice Richison c   6 Dec.

[Fol. 67b].

Will. Shephard entered Parish Clerk of Horncastle in the year of our Lord God one thousand seven Hundred and Twenty five, February the 23d.

September the 28th 1662.

Memorand'm the day and yeere above written that the Booke of Common Prayer lately sett forth By the Authority of the Kings Matie & his court was Read in the p'sh Church of Horncastle by me Thomas Gibson Vicar there, & freely & willingly assented unto according to an Act of Parliament in that case made & p'vided. In witness whereof the said Mr. Gibson with other of the Inhabitants whose names are hereunto subscribed have set their hands.

Tho : Gibson, Vicar.
John Harding, parrish Clerk.

Imprim. given by Robert Clarke of new dowood to the poor of Horncastle the sum of ten shillings for ever to be payed yearly upon St Thomas Day out of his land in Thimbleby.

It. given by Mrs Ann Smith of Horncastle widdow formerly the wife of Mr John Betham the yearly legacie of twenty shillings to the poor of Horncastle to be paid out of the lands of the said John Betham wh came by the right of the said Ann to continue for ever.

The Gift of Mr Thomas Bromely June 6th 1661.

Item. I give to the poore people of Horncastle fforty shillings per ann to be payed out of my lands in Haltham upon Bayne to be payed by the present terant to the overseers of the poore of Horncastle.

It. given by Mr George Acham of Asterby the sum of one hundred & fforty poundes to purchase certain lands the Ann' rent thereof to be and to remaine to the use of the poore of Horncastle for ever.

It. Given by Mr Thomas Gibson Vicar of Horncastle a hearse cloath for the beire for the use of the Towne of Horncastle January the 10th 1671.

[End of Second Register Book.]